Ruth Leimenzon Engles

Written in a Barn

The Diary of a Young Woman from Vilna

This publication was supported by
**The Moshe Mirilashvili Center for Research on
The Holocaust in the Soviet Union**

Ruth Leimenzon Engles

WRITTEN IN A BARN

The Diary of a Young Woman from Vilna

Translated from the Yiddish by David Engles

Edited by Ben-Tsiyon Klibansky

יד ושם
YAD VASHEM
THE WORLD HOLOCAUST
REMEMBRANCE CENTER

THE INTERNATIONAL INSTITUTE
FOR HOLOCAUST RESEARCH

The Moshe Mirilashvili Center for Research on
The Holocaust in the Soviet Union

Ruth Leimenzon Engelshtern

Farshribn in a shayer

Language and Production Editor: Dania Valdez

P.O.B. 3477, Jerusalem 9103401, Israel
publications.marketing@yadvashem.org.il
First published in Yiddish by the Ghetto Fighters' House, 1973

ISBN 978-965-308-684-5

Typesetting: Hava Salzman
Printed in Israel by Printiv Press, Jerusalem

In loving memory of our parents,
Ruth Engles, Lazar Engles, Lenke Malek, and Jacob Malek,
who survived the Holocaust and became the victors,
triumphing over the destroyers
by having the courage and conviction
to continue to observe the traditions of Judaism
and to transmit them to their descendants.

CONTENTS

My Mother's Legacy

by David Engles

On June 22, 1941, the Nazis invaded Lithuania, occupied Vilna, set up a ghetto, and murdered almost all of the Vilna Jews during the next two years. My mother, Ruth Leimenzon Engles, managed to survive and, just before the liquidation of the ghetto in September 1943, she was able to escape and find a hiding place in a barn on a farm a few kilometers outside of Vilna, where she hid for ten months. During the last two months in the barn, she wrote a diary describing her three-year ordeal—over two years under the Nazi occupation of Vilna and then ten months, from September 1943 to July 1944, in the barn.

My father, Lazar Engles,[1] who married my mother after the war, kept the diary safe and brought it to Israel when he retired and made *aliya* in 1968. A few years later, in 1972, the diary was published in Yiddish with the title *Farshribn in a shayer* (Written in A Barn) by the Ghetto Fighters' House, which is in a kibbutz near Haifa. The original manuscript is kept in the archives of the Ghetto Fighters' House.[2]

My mother died in the summer of 1955. She was just forty-five years old. I was nine years old and was away at a summer camp when she passed away. I never got a chance to say goodbye to her, and even worse than that, to my great regret and loss, I never got a chance to discover what an

---

1 Lazar Engles' original last name was Engelstern (transliterated from Yiddish as Engelshtern). It was changed to Engles when the family became U.S. citizens.

2 I received a copy of the original when my wife, Eva, and I visited there a number of years ago.

exceptional person she was. Many years later, in 2002, when I was fifty-six years old, I spent half a year diligently and carefully translating from Yiddish into English the diary that she had written in 1944. That is when I came to appreciate what a truly remarkable person my mother was.

The diary is an extraordinary document. It was written by my mother in the spring of 1944, after enduring a very cold, harsh winter in an environment where discovery of her hideout meant certain death at the hands of the Nazis or collaborators. It is a powerful narrative in which my mother, not knowing if she will survive, reveals her deepest thoughts and feelings, as she describes how she survived—using her intelligence and common sense, and helped by luck and perhaps miracles. She was thirty-four years old at the time, and her perspective is that of a mature woman.

The diary may be viewed from three perspectives. First, it is my mother's own personal story of how she survived by strength of will and unwavering fortitude. In these pages, she bares her soul as she writes down her personal thoughts, ideas, and feelings about everything she has lived through and is still living through in the barn.

Second, the diary recounts an interesting and suspenseful story as my mother describes her escape from the ghetto, just before its liquidation, with the help of the wife of her former boss, as well as her daily life in the barn, never knowing if she will survive the danger that lurks just outside the barn door.

Third, the diary is also an important and unique historical document. It is the only diary written by a mature woman about the Vilna ghetto.[3] In it, my mother describes many aspects of life in the ghetto during her two years there, from June 1941 to September 1943. She comments about the Jews, the Germans, the Lithuanians, the Judenrat, the Jewish police, and the various classes of people that emerged in the ghetto. Her descriptions are so vivid that the reader feels as if he himself is there with her. Her comments and observations about the people whom she writes about reflect deep, psychological insight.

---

3 A reconstructed diary by Maria Rolnikaite (Masha Rolnik), a girl from Vilna, first released in Lithuanian as *Turiu papasakoti* (Vilna: Valstybine Politines ir Mokslines Literaturos Leidykla, 1963), was published in English recently. See Maria Rolnikaite, *I Must Tell* (n.p.: Lulu Press, 2018).

The story that my mother relates of how she survived, of how she never gave up and never lost hope is truly inspirational. There are many passages in the diary that reflect her amazingly positive attitude about life, even in the darkest circumstances. The following excerpt clearly exemplifies this attitude. It was written on July 4, 1944, when the Soviets were on the verge of liberating Vilna, and my mother was now thinking about a future life, which until then she had not even thought would become a reality.

> My desires are not at all very great. I want only to have a tranquil life, without aggravation. I cannot imagine what that will look like. But it does happen that the impossible becomes possible. Who could have ever imagined it to be possible that in one day, not even twenty-four hours, all of Vilna's Jews could be confined in one little corner? And then that in the course of two years Vilna would be completely "liberated" of such a dense well-established Jewish population that had been there for hundreds of years? If that can happen, then it could also happen that something, which today seems impossible to me, might become possible. I must believe this and not question it.

My mother's words also reflect the universal experience of Holocaust survivors. Many of the survivors did not want to speak about their Holocaust experiences. The following paragraph may provide an insight into the reluctance of survivors to talk about what they suffered and what they lost. This paragraph was also written on July 4, 1944.

> If indeed I live to see the Soviets and crawl out of here to the free world, then I must completely make myself over, wipe out entirely all sentimental feeling. I have to forget everything and everyone, just as if nothing and nobody had ever existed in the world until now. I have to accept everything with a good-natured spirit, without a sense of tragedy. Only in this way is it possible for me to continue to exist. It is a difficult task, and I have doubts as to whether I can pull it off.

A few years after the diary was published, my father published two books, both also written in Yiddish. His first book, *In ghettos un velder* (In

Ghettos and Forests),[4] tells the story of his survival during the Holocaust: how he escaped from the Vilna ghetto, how he survived the infamous Lida death march that resulted in the death of over 5,000 Jews, and how he eventually joined the Bielski partisan camp in the forests of Belorussia and became the cook there. His second book, *Mit di vegn fun der sheyris-hapleyte* (On the Way with the Holocaust Survivors),[5] is his autobiography in which he relates the details of his life from the summer of 1944, when he left the forest and returned to Vilna, until 1976, when he was living in Israel after having made *aliya* from the United States in 1968.

My father and mother knew each other before the Nazis came and destroyed their lives. My father lost his wife and two young daughters, and many other close relatives. My mother lost her husband and also many other members of her family. They knew each other well before the war, because my father and my mother's husband had been friends since their school days. After the Soviet liberation, both of them returned to Vilna—my father from the forest and my mother from the barn—and one day by chance they met. Here is my father's description of that meeting, as it appears in his autobiography in a chapter titled "Ruth Leimenzon and Her Diary."

> Three dark years had gone by. One day, I came to the community courtyard at 19 German Street and I met Ruth. Is it possible to imagine the joy we both felt? After all, we knew each other well, having socialized with her and her husband on various occasions. They had lived near us, and we had often visited each other. From then on, we would meet almost every day.

The chapter continues with a passage that stunned me when I first read it. The diary, more than providing me with insights into the kind of person my mother was, had actually played an even more important role in my

---

4 Leizer Engelshtern, *In ghettos un velder* (Yiddish) (Tel Aviv: Hakibbutz Hame'uhad, 1972). Yad Vashem will publish the English translation of *In ghettos un velder* in the near future, and I hope that my father's autobiography will also be published in English one day.

5 Leizer Engelshtern, *Mit di vegn fun der sheyris-hapleyte* (Yiddish) (Tel Aviv: Igud Yotze Vilna Vehaseviva BeYisrael, 1976).

life. When I read the passage, it suddenly occurred to me that perhaps I owe my very existence to the diary. The passage begins as follows.

> From the very first day that Ruth met me, there awoke in her a hope to begin life anew. She did not hide this from me and was open in telling me that she was prepared to bind her fate to mine. I understood her well and felt her loneliness, although very differently, within me. The reason was that my thought process flowed in the opposite direction from that of my friend's wife, Ruth. I was of the opinion that it was still too soon to begin anew, especially when I still didn't know what would become of me. My first priority was to escape from the shadow of Ponary,[6] no matter what the cost, and to reach the free world.

The passage continues as my father quotes the following entry in my mother's diary, dated July 17, 1944, just a few days after the liberation of Vilna. It is the next to last entry in the diary.

> A heaviness presses in on me. How does one start life all over again? Loneliness terrifies me. Where to go? What to do? Maybe I will find acquaintances, friends. But that's not it. I know how it feels to be among people and yet feel lonely. I don't need much. I just need one person.[7]

And then my father wrote: "After reading these lines, I thought about them for a while, and soon her last four words compelled me to consider that maybe these lines have a close connection to me?" So, he decided to marry Ruth, and they had a son, and that son, namely me, might never have been born had the diary not been written.

After getting married in Vilna in 1944, my parents joined the stream of Holocaust survivors wandering through Europe, eventually ending up in the Cinecittà DP[8] Camp in Rome, Italy, which is where I was born in

---

6 Ponary was an area located just a few kilometers outside of Vilna. It was the murder site where the Nazis took the Vilna Jews to be killed by their willing and enthusiastic Lithuanian helpers.

7 In Yiddish: ikh darf nor eynem.

8 Displaced Persons.

1946. Three years later, we immigrated to the United States and settled in New York City on 187th Street in Washington Heights.

Not long after we moved into Washington Heights, another young child, Eva Malek, came to live a few blocks away on 189th Street. Eva, who has been my lovely, extraordinary, wise, and creative wife for the last fifty-one years, has a family background that is in many ways similar to mine. Her parents were from Kosice, Czechoslovakia. They also knew each other before the war. They also lost their loved ones. Eva's mother lost her husband and many close relatives, including her parents and a brother. Her father lost his wife and three children, and many close relatives, including his parents and siblings. They also suffered in the Nazi hell. Her mother survived Auschwitz. Her father survived the Nazi forced labor camps. They also met after the war and decided to start life anew. They had two children—her brother, Andre, and Eva. After spending some time in a DP camp in Austria, the Malek family immigrated to the United States. It was my great fortune that they settled in Washington Heights, where destiny guaranteed that I would one day meet my *basherte* (soulmate) Eva.

The four people whose lives were torn apart during the Holocaust, my parents and Eva's parents, are part of a group referred to as "survivors." Eva and I have spoken to various groups about our parents' experiences. In Eva's words:

> Because they had the courage and conviction to continue with their lives, raising their children in a traditional Jewish home, they are not merely survivors, they are victors. And all the millions of Jews living today, who are descendants of the Holocaust survivors, are a testament to the statement that they are all victors. Whenever the world tries to eliminate us, we come back even stronger.

Today, the descendants from our parents number over forty individuals over four generations. From the first generation of three children—Eva, her brother, Andre, and me—has come a second generation of five grandchildren, and then a third generation of twenty-six great grandchildren, and a fourth still growing generation of nine great, great grandchildren. Every single one of them is an observant Jew.

My family—me, Eva, our two children, nine grandsons, six granddaughters, and one great grandson—are all residents of Israel. Had Israel existed during the time of the Nazis, 6 million Jews would not have perished. Today, the world is again experiencing a rise in antisemitism, and the existence of Israel assures a safe haven for any Jew who may need one. For Eva and me, the rebirth of Israel as the Jewish homeland represents the victory of the Jewish nation over all her enemies, both past and present.

It was very important for my father to keep the memory of Vilna alive and to do everything possible to not let the world forget the tragedy of the Holocaust. That is why he wrote his two books. That is why, recognizing what a unique and important document my mother's diary was, he took upon himself the mission to tell her story by getting the original Yiddish diary published. In the following excerpt from his autobiography, he beautifully expresses the satisfaction he felt in accomplishing this goal:

> One day Ruth showed me a dense, handwritten notebook that she had written while in her hiding place. When I finished reading her diary, I told her to protect it, like her own eyes, because this document about the horrible period was an important contribution to the history of the Holocaust.
>
> Throughout the entire time of our life together and also after she died, I set for myself a goal that this tragic and extremely important document about the Holocaust period would receive recognition. All my thoughts were focused in this direction— that this "*Megilat Ruth*" would see the light of day and would be made available to the public. The publication of her diary is for me and for our son, David, the greatest satisfaction, and also our garland of flowers on the grave of the prematurely deceased author of *Written in a Barn*.

I am proud to continue my father's mission of making my mother's story known to a wider public. I share this satisfaction with my soulmate and life partner, Eva, who has provided invaluable advice and suggestions in developing presentations for various groups and has participated with me in making these presentations in which we tell the story of our parents' survival during the Holocaust. I am deeply grateful and thankful to Eva for all her support and encouragement throughout our years together, and I feel extraordinarily fortunate to have her as my wife.

With the publication of the English translation of my mother's diary, we both now have the satisfaction of placing a second "garland of flowers" to memorialize my mother's words.

Historical Preface

by Ben-Tsiyon Klibansky

Ruth Leimenzon Engelshtern (Engles) began writing her diary in Yiddish about two months before the liberation of the city of Vilna and its environs from the hands of the Germans. She wrote this diary under very difficult conditions inside a barn in a remote village not far from the township of Niementchin in Vilna County, where she was constantly in danger of death. The diary served as a means of passing the time, or in her words, "pushing time," and as somebody to talk to: "At times, it seems to me like I am having a conversation with someone."[9] In this diary she described, almost daily, events that took place from May 15 to July 19, 1944.

Ruth's description of these events contributes to the knowledge and understanding of the historical occurrences and of the relations between the Jews and the peasants in the county of Vilna at the end of the war, as well as to the study of the mindset, actions, and reactions of a Jewish woman who was in hiding in a confined space inside a barn for many months, waiting for the war to end. However, the diary assumes even greater importance due to the integration of another key element: While writing the diary, Ruth recalled many incidences that had occurred in Vilna since the outbreak of the war, which she associated with the daily occurrences. She did not overlook almost any

---

9 In contrast to other writers of Vilna diaries written during the Holocaust, she did not aspire to tell others about the atrocities of the Germans and the Lithuanians toward the Jews, or to record the history of the exact occurrences of the Vilna ghetto for the next generations. See Mark Dworzecki, "Yomanei Ghetto Vilna," in Mordechai Eli'av, ed., *Iyunim BiTekufat HaShoah* (Hebrew) (Jerusalem: Bar-Ilan University, 1980), pp. 86–88.

important detail in the life of the Jews in the city until their complete annihilation.[10] Thus she wrote about what happened to her in the first days and weeks of the war and then about how she survived in Ghetto II, the "Small Ghetto," and finally about her life and her daily struggle in Ghetto I, the "Large Ghetto."

Her diary includes an account of her rescue, her escape from Ghetto II a week before its liquidation in October 1941, her subsequent escape from Ghetto I two days before the liquidation in September 1943, and her ensuing experiences in hiding, whether in the house of an urban Polish Christian woman in Vilna for a week at a time, or in a barn of a Christian peasant in the remote village of Simanuvka for many months. Her diary is therefore a combination of a traditional diary in which she chronologically describes local events and encounters with the peasants in the village, and a personal testimony about significant events in the Vilna ghetto throughout its existence, written while they were very fresh in her memory.

Although the personal testimony of these events does not add greatly to our historical knowledge, its uniqueness is in the analysis by the writer, a married, mature woman in her early thirties, of the events and the participants—Germans, Lithuanians, Poles, and especially Jews—with the objectivity of the distance of time—a year, two years, and even three years after the events themselves.

Ruth survived, returned to ruined Vilna, married Leizer Engelshtern (Lazar Engles), himself a survivor and a partisan, and after a few years in a DP camp in Italy, where her son was born, she immigrated to the United States in 1949 with her family. However, she did not live there for long. She passed away in 1955.[11]

Ruth kept her original diary with her throughout all her wanderings. It is preserved today in the archives of the Ghetto Fighters' House, which published it in 1972–1973. This book is a translation from Yiddish into English by the writer's son, Dr. David Engles, of that first edition.

---

10 Therefore, it is surprising that the writer did not mention explicitly the *Selektionen* of the provincial Jews by the Vilna Jewish police in the beginning of April 1943 and especially the Wittenberg incident on July 16, 1943.

11 For her detailed history after the liberation, see Engelshtern, *Mit Di Vegn*, pp. 144–331.

Written under inhumane conditions in a dark hideout, the diary reflects the writer's state of mind. Indeed, Ruth wrote the diary for personal purposes and did not intend for it to be read by others. Thus many of the people whom she mentions in the diary are referred to by last name or first name only. Although the public figures among them were easily identified, it was more difficult to identify private individuals. Thanks to the combination of clues and other signs in the diary and to archival documentation, it was possible to identify some of them. However, this approach of brevity and allusion in the writer's writing is not limited only to people's names but is especially evident in cases where she mentions incidents in the ghetto. Noting them only for the purpose of expressing her opinion of them and the feelings that they evoked in her, she did not detail them. Footnotes with short explanations from research books, memoirs, or other diaries have been added to make it easier for the reader to understand to what historical events the author is referring.

The problem, however, is that these historical events appear in the diary in a completely associative way. With a stroke of a pen, Ruth spans long distances of many months and even years. For a reader who is not well acquainted with the events of the Holocaust period in Vilna, the footnotes are not sufficient to follow the writer's intentions. In order to make it easier for the reader to get acquainted with the tangle of occurrences in the ghetto as described in the diary, the order of the events is presented on a chronological timeline in Section One of this preface. Here, too, the task of creating an orderly timeline of the events that occurred in Vilna during the war, which seems ostensibly simple, was actually more complex, since there is quite a bit of ambiguity and not a few contradictions among the memoirs and other diaries. Therefore, when required, the most recent study on the Vilna ghetto, published in 2013 by the late Dr. Aharon Einat (Zalkind), a survivor of the ghetto, served as a reference.[12]

Following the presentation of the main events in the Vilna ghetto in chronological order, it is possible to turn attention to getting to know the writer in the context of those events and how she dealt with them, as presented in Section Two of this preface. The information presented there

12 Aharon Einat, *Hayei Yom-Yom BeGhetto Vilna* (Hebrew) (Haifa: Moreshet, 2013).

about Ruth is, of course, based on her diary, as well as on supplementary archival material.

After Ruth's escape from Ghetto I prior to its liquidation and after finding temporary shelter with a Polish Christian woman in the city, she hid in the remote village of Simanuvka for another ten months. This period, which seems to be stable and colorless, is also rich in twists and turns that are difficult to follow because of the associative nature of Ruth's writing. Moreover, from the beginning of her diary, she counted the days that had passed from her arrival in the village, as well as from the event of her last bath in the farmer's house. Because of a mistake that she sometimes made regarding the date of her departure from the ghetto—attributing her departure to August 1943 instead of September 1943—she erred in calculating the days and months. Although these errors have been corrected in the footnotes, here too it is appropriate to construct an orderly timetable. Therefore, Section Three of this preface also presents a chronological timeline of events in the village.

The associative structure of the diary makes it difficult to divide it into chapters and under headings and subheadings. Moreover, the allusive language of the diary in mentioning Ruth's acquaintances also does not justify adding a search index of people to this publication. Instead, Section Four of this preface presents a kind of orientation index, which makes it easier for the reader to find events of interest in the diary, according to the entry in the diary in which they are described, or according to the dates of the events.

It seems most appropriate to conclude this historical preface with a word about the uniqueness of this diary regarding Ruth's approach to the governing institutions of the ghetto. This approach, which is presented in Section Five, is sometimes very critical but also very balanced, because of her mature consideration of the constraints.

Finally, as an editor, I cannot refrain from relating personally to the diary. I spent my childhood in the alleyways of Vilna, only two decades after the complete annihilation of its Jewish inhabitants, including my many relatives. Reading the diary seems to take me back to those childhood districts. My home, as well as my kindergarten, stood in what had been in the not-too-distant past the western end of Ghetto II. Before my eyes, I can still see the image of a tall and menacing wall standing in the kindergarten compound, which even then, as a small child, appeared to me to be a dilapidated remnant of a destroyed building. The diary seems to make it very clear why this was so. To go to my school, which was not within the former Ghetto II boundaries, it was necessary to step out of our large courtyard compound and cross a bright and wide street that not accidentally was then, as it is now, called the Wide Street. However, the diary does not evoke only buildings and streets. The attitude of the Lithuanians toward their Jewish neighbors, as described in the diary, also did not disappear after the war. I recall feeling echoes of it in the expressions of some of my companions, probably sons of those murderous Lithuanians from the war. For me, the diary is therefore not only a historical source for studying the events in Jewish Vilna during the war, but also in a sense a book of my prehistory.

It is my hope that this book will be another important contribution to an understanding of the complex history of the Vilna ghetto, and that it will serve to acquaint readers with the unique and fascinating paths of survivors from loss to salvation.

Section One: Chronology of the Events in Vilna

From the point of view of the Jews of Vilna, the history of the city from the beginning of Operation Barbarossa to the liquidation of the ghetto and of its Jewish residents may be divided into the following main periods:

(1) Absence of Government: June 22–23, 1941
(2) Temporary Governments: June 24–August 1, 1941
(3) German Civil Administration: August 2–September 5, 1941
(4) Existence of Two Ghettos: September 6–October 21, 1941
(5) *Aktionen* in Ghetto I: October 22–December 23, 1941
(6) Stability in the Ghetto: December 24, 1941–August 5, 1943
(7) Deportations to Estonia: August 6–September 4, 1943
(8) Liquidation of the Ghetto: September 5–24, 1943

Absence of Government: June 22–23, 1941

At the outbreak of the war on June 22, 1941, about 60,000 Jews lived in Vilna.[13] That morning began with the thunder of bombs dropping from the sky, which caused great panic among the inhabitants of the city. The Soviet army and officials in the Soviet government undertook urgent evacuation efforts from Vilna. Jews, especially young people, also tried to flee to the borders, including in carts and on foot.[14] However, even the few who managed to reach the border did not receive a permit to cross it and were forced to return. Meanwhile, Lithuanian gangs began abusing and killing Soviet soldiers and their families,[15] and especially Jews.

Temporary Governments: June 24–August 1, 1941

On June 24, 1941, the German army entered Vilna. In the early days, a joint German–Lithuanian government operated in the city, and the Germans recognized the institutions that the Lithuanians had captured or established. On July 2, however, the joint rule ended, and the Lithuanian institutions were abolished or transferred to the direct command of the German military government. From then on, the Lithuanian units, army, and police operated only within German frameworks. During this period, which lasted a month, the Germans imposed harsh decrees on the Jewish residents, while denying them their rights and, at the same time, they began seizing men to kill them in death pits in Ponary.[16] The

13 Herman Kruk, *The Last Days: Chronicles from the Vilna Ghetto and the Camps, 1939–1944* (New Haven: YIVO and Yale University Press, 2002), p. 284; see also Einat, *Hayei Yom-Yom*, pp. 103n59.

14 See for example, Yitzhak Rudashevski, *Yomano Shel Na'ar MiVilna* (Hebrew) (Tel Aviv: Hakibbutz Hame'uhad, 1976), p. 13; Reizl Korchak, *Lehavot Ba'efer* (Haifa: Moreshet, 1965), pp. 8–9; Yehezkel Kremerman, *MiVilna "Yerushalayim DeLita" Ad Haifa* (Hebrew) (Haifa: Yehezkel Kremerman, 1995), p. 57.

15 Rudashevski, *Yomano Shel Na'ar MiVilna*, p. 13.

16 Ponary was a resort area, about 8 kilometers from Vilna, to the right of the Vilna–Warsaw train line. Beginning on July 11, 1941, this was the murder site. See Szmerke Kaczerginski, *Churbn Vilna* (Yiddish) (New York: Fareinikter Vilner Hilfs-Komitet, 1947), pp. 14, 29. Almost 70,000 Jews from Vilna and the surrounding areas were shot there and later removed from the mass graves and burned in pyres.

unit that carried out the capture and murder of the Jews at that time was Einsatzkommando 9, which incorporated about 150 Lithuanians from the Ypatingasis būrys (Vilnian Special Squad) into its ranks.[17] These Lithuanians formed the main execution force that was primarily responsible for rounding up Jews from the city streets.

As the Jews began to shut themselves in their homes and to hide, the searches and abductions moved to the homes themselves. The hostages were taken to Lukishki Prison,[18] and from there to Ponary. A special operation was carried out on July 17, 1941, in the Novogrod suburb. Jewish men caught in their apartments were gathered in the market square, where they were tortured and then transported in trucks to Lukishki Prison, and from there to Ponary.[19] During the month of July, 5,000 Jews were murdered, most of them men.[20] The Jews were also ordered to establish a Judenrat during this period. Its main job was to provide labor on demand, but it served to address the plight of the Jews as well.

German Civil Administration: August 2–September 5, 1941

On August 2, 1941, the German military administration was replaced by a German civil administration, headed by Hans Christian Hingst. Franz Murer was entrusted the responsibility for Jewish affairs.[21] The municipal Lithuanian government also dealt with the Jews of Vilna—along with the

---

17 Ypatingasis būrys (Special Squad), which was formed by the German occupational forces, was initially a subordinate of Einsatzkommando 9. Its members, primarily composed of Lithuanian volunteers recruited from the former members of the paramilitary Lithuanian Riflemen's Union, snatched Jews in the streets, seized Jews from their apartments, and participated in their massacres in Ponary.

18 Lukishki Prison was located in the Lukishki suburb, northwest to the Old City of Vilna.

19 According to Mark Dworzecki, almost 700 Jews were then dragged out of their houses; see Mark Dworzecki, *Yerushalayim DeLita in kamf un umkum* (Yiddish) (Paris: Yiddishn Natzionaln Arbeter-Farband in Amerike un Yiddishn Folksfarband in Frankraich, 1948), pp. 32–34. Korchak wrote that 500 Jews were taken that day; see Korchak, *Lehavot Ba'efer*, p. 12.

20 Einat, *Hayei Yom-Yom*, p. 83.

21 Franz Murer (1912–1994), a Nazi officer and right hand man of the regional commissar of Vilna, Hans Christian Hingst, was in charge of Jewish affairs and an "expert on Jewish questions."

German authorities. At the same time, independent SS units continued to operate in the city, and they directly carried out the murder of Jews.

On August 6, 1941, the German government imposed a ransom of 5 million rubles on the Jews, charging members of the Judenrat to personally implement the order. The Judenrat was able to collect large sums of money and numerous valuables, but since they did not reach the required amount on time, the Germans eased their terms a little.

At the end of August, the administration began preparations for the establishment of a ghetto in the city. To this end, it executed a planned provocation on August 31, 1941, in which German soldiers were allegedly shot in an ambush by Jews, two of whom were captured.[22] The provocation served as an excuse to expel all the Jews who lived on the streets near the shooting site from their houses. There were many members of the Judenrat among the deportees who were transferred to Lukishki Prison and from there taken to their deaths in Ponary. About 5,000 Jews were murdered, including women and children.[23]

Existence of Two Ghettos: September 6–October 21, 1941

After the old quarter of Vilna was emptied of its Jewish inhabitants, and the few Poles who lived there were ordered to leave, the Germans were able to establish the ghetto there. They actually created two ghettos: Ghetto I, the "large ghetto," whose entrance was on Rudnitzki Street, and Ghetto II, the "small ghetto," whose gate was on Gaon Street. On Saturday, September 6, 1941, Germans and Lithuanians arrived at the homes of the Jews in the city and ordered everyone to leave with their luggage. The Jews were hastily led by Lithuanians in two separate directions, toward the two ghettos. However, some Jews, approximately 4,000, were taken directly to Lukishki Prison, and approximately 2,000 were led first to Lida Alley and then to Lukishki Prison. From there, they were taken to Ponary.[24]

---

22 The actual shooters were Lithuanian policemen. This provocation was named "The First Great Provocation."

23 Kruk, *The Last Days*, p. 83; Einat, *Hayei Yom-Yom*, p. 93.

24 Einat, *Hayei Yom-Yom*, pp. 99, 103. According to A. Sutzkever, the Jews from Lida Alley were taken directly to Ponary. Jews called this "The Second Great Provocation." See

By the time the deportees entered the ghettos, about 20,000 Jews had been murdered.[25] The remaining population of Vilna Jewry, about 40,000 people, were confined in those two ghettos—about 30,000 in Ghetto I, and about 10,000 in Ghetto II.[26] Ghetto I included the following streets: Rudnitzki, Shpitol, Zavalne, Shavl, Strashun, and some courtyards on Disna Street, Lida Alley, Yatkever Street, Konske Street, and Carmelites Street.[27] Ghetto II included the streets of Glezer, Yatkever, Yiddishe, the beginning of Gaon, and some very small alleys near the *Shulheif* (synagogue courtyard).

The Jews thought that the ghetto would protect them from the abductions and abuses by the Poles and the Lithuanians; the local non-Jews also made this clear to them.[28] However, the concentration of Jews in the ghettos made it easier for the Germans to carry out *Aktionen* and to dilute the Jewish population in Vilna. Ghetto I was intended for craftsmen and other skilled people and their families, while Ghetto II was for unskilled and unemployed people, who had no right to exist in the eyes of the Germans. Since the Jews were transferred to the ghettos without any order or preliminary examination, the Germans' goal at that stage was to make the necessary demographic changes with the aim of eventually leaving only one ghetto active: Ghetto I with its population of skilled workers and their families.

The implementation of the German plan began on September 15, 1941. That day about 3,500 unemployed people were taken out of Ghetto I on the pretext that they were being transferred to Ghetto II,[29] but only 600

Abraham Sutzkever, *Vilner ghetto 1941–1944* (Yiddish) (Paris: Farband fun di Vilner in Frankraich, 1946), p. 50.

25 Kruk, *The Last Days*, p. 285. Einat estimated the number as 16,000; see Einat, *Hayei Yom-Yom*, pp. 103n59, 108.

26 Kruk, *The Last Days*, p. 285; Dworzecki, *Yerushalayim DeLita*, p. 140.

27 Later, more courtyards on Disna Street, Yatkever Street, Oshmener Street, and German Street were added to the ghetto.

28 Mendel Balberyshski, *Shtarker fun ayzn* (Yiddish) (Tel Aviv: Hamenora, 1967), pp. 178; Engelshtern, *In ghettos un velder*, p. 10.

29 Kruk, *The Last Days*, p. 112. According to Balberyshski, their number was 2,000. He also claimed that the original intention of the Germans was to carry out this *Aktion* in Ghetto II, but due to the preventive activity of the Judenrat of this ghetto, the *Aktion* was transferred to Ghetto I. See Balberyshski, *Shtarker fun ayzn*, pp. 195, 256.

of them arrived there; the rest were sent to Ponary. That *Aktion* shattered the illusion that the ghetto was a safe place for the Jews.[30] In another *Aktion*, conducted in Ghetto I on the evening of Yom Kippur, October 1, 1941, 2,200 people were driven out.[31] That same day, a series of *Aktionen* were initiated in Ghetto II with the aim of liquidating it. During the first, carried out on Yom Kippur, 1,700 people were evicted. It was followed by other *Aktionen*—2,000 people were forced out on October 3–4; 3,000 people on October 16;[32] and 2,500 people during the last *Aktion* on October 21, resulting in the liquidation of Ghetto II.[33]

Aktionen in Ghetto I: October 22—December 23, 1941

As mentioned, Ghetto I was intended for skilled workers. To this end, the Germans issued 3,000 *Gelbscheine* (yellow permits) to live in the ghetto, which allowed a wife and two children at most to be registered on each permit.[34] Thus, a maximum of about 12,000 people could officially live in the ghetto. Indeed, on October 24, 1941, the first *Gelbschein-Aktion* was carried out, and more than 5,000 unlicensed people were removed from the ghetto.[35]

Another *Aktion* took place in Ghetto I at the end of October at the provocation of the Judenrat and the Jewish police, which announced that

---

30 Ibid., p. 256.

31 It was a trap for work permit holders, who were ordered to come to the gate to sign these permits; see Kruk, *The Last Days*, p. 285.

32 These last two *Aktionen* are not mentioned in the diary.

33 A few *malinas* (hideouts) that were not discovered remained in the ghetto. Regarding the numbers, see Kruk, *The Last Days*, p. 285. Kruk cited the date of the last *Aktion* as October 29, which Einat corrected to October 21; see Einat, *Hayei Yom-Yom*, p. 104.

34 Dworzecki, *Yerushalayim DeLita*, p. 101. According to Balberyshski, the Germans issued a total of 3,500 permits, which could have provided protection for up to 14,000 Jews; see Balberyshski, *Shtarker fun ayzn*, pp. 260, 266. The biological relationship between those registered on a permit was not specifically examined. Those registered got blue passes that together with the yellow permit should have served as life passes. On the night of December 21, 1941, the ghetto police issued pink permits to those registered on a yellow permit holding blue passes, who stayed in the ghetto. These pink permits, which were only valid inside the ghetto, were also issued to a few others, who were needed to work in the ghetto.

35 Kruk, *The Last Days*, p. 285; Rudashevski, *Yomano Shel Na'ar MiVilna*, p. 25.

anyone who wanted a vacant apartment could move with their belongings to the empty Ghetto II. Indeed, many of the unlicensed moved to this ghetto. The police also began forcibly moving the elderly and the sick to Ghetto II. A few days later, Lithuanians arrived there and took everyone to Ponary.[36]

On November 3, 1941, the second *Gelbschein-Aktion* began. The licensed occupants of Ghetto I were transferred to the empty Ghetto II, while some remained in their workplaces. A search began for the unlicensed occupants in Ghetto I, and the captives were transferred to Ponary. At the end of this three-day *Aktion* in which 1,200 people were found, the residents of Ghetto I were allowed to return to their previous apartments.[37] Other small-scale *Aktionen* were conducted in the ghetto until December 21, 1941.[38]

Stability in the Ghetto: December 24, 1941–August 5, 1943

The period of stability in the ghetto began on December 24, 1941. More than 12,000 "official" Jews, almost all of them registered on yellow permits, resided in Ghetto I.[39] The unlicensed people began to leave their hideouts and, in the course of time, the Jews who had fled from Belorussia, or from towns in the county of Vilna whose congregations had been annihilated, arrived in the ghetto, adding another 5,000 people to the Jewish population there.[40]

---

36 Balberyshski, *Shtarker fun ayzn*, pp. 278–279; Kremerman, *MiVilna "Yerushalayim DeLita,"* pp. 84–85; Rudashevski, *Yomano Shel Na'ar MiVilna*, pp. 25–26, 29. This *Aktion* is not mentioned in the diary.

37 Several hundred Jews who had hidden in *malinas* in Ghetto II since its liquidation returned with them; see Dworzecki, *Yerushalayim DeLita*, pp. 121–122. Regarding the numbers, see Kruk, *The Last Days*, p. 285.

38 Kruk, *The Last Days*, p. 286. According to Sutzkever, "The Pink *Scheinen Aktion*," which began on December 21, 1941, lasted three days and resulted in the capture of almost 1,000 Jews who did not have pink permits; Sutzkever, *Vilner ghetto* p. 54.

39 Kruk, *The Last Days*, p. 286.

40 Dworzecki, *Yerushalayim DeLita*, p. 141. According to Einat, there were 20,000 Jews living in the ghetto during the period of stability; Einat, *Hayei Yom-Yom*, p. 106.

On April 5, 1943, an unusual *Aktion* was carried out. The ghetto police went to the nearby towns of Svientchian, Oshmene, Michalishek, and Svir to conduct *Selektionen* there. Those unqualified for work were immediately annihilated, while the rest were sent by train to the Kovno ghetto.[41] Vilna ghetto inhabitants who had originally arrived from Kovno, or who had recently come from the surrounding towns, were also given the opportunity to join those on the trains to Kovno.[42] However, these trains halted in Ponary, and all the passengers, about 4,000 Jews, were massacred.[43] What was special about this *Aktion* was that the next day Jewish policemen were taken to Ponary to collect the corpses of the Jews who had attempted to escape and were scattered over a large area. These policemen were allowed to return to the ghetto, and although they were forbidden to relate what they saw, the news leaked and the entire ghetto learned about what was really happening in Ponary.[44] Moreover, a few days later the Germans themselves sent the clothes of the murdered to the needy in the ghetto. For the first time since the ghetto was established, the Germans showed the Jews what Ponary was. By then, almost 50,000 Jews from Vilna and its surroundings had been murdered there. However, until then no German had ever disclosed what had actually happened to those Jews.[45]

Deportations to Estonia: August 6–September 4, 1943

When the Vilna ghetto was condemned to destruction,[46] the Germans began a series of rapid deportations of the ghetto inhabitants to labor camps in Estonia. Some of the deportees were seized by the Germans,

---

41 These details are not mentioned in the diary.

42 According to Einat, 350 Jews were sent to the Kovno ghetto; Einat, *Hayei Yom-Yom*, p. 314. Balberyshski did not specify their number; see Balberyshski, *Shtarker fun ayzn*, p. 455.

43 Kruk, *The Last Days*, pp. 500–501; Einat, *Hayei Yom-Yom*, p. 315.

44 Even before that, testimonies were collected from women and children who managed to escape the death pits of Ponary, but the ghetto Jews refused to believe their stories.

45 Balberyshski, *Shtarker fun ayzn*, p. 456.

46 Himmler issued the order to liquidate the ghettos in *Ostland* on June 21, 1943; Yitzhak Arad, *Vilna HaYehudit BeMa'avak UveChilayon* (Hebrew) (Tel-Aviv: Yad Vashem and Tel-Aviv University and Po'alim Library Press, 1976), pp. 321–322.

some volunteered to be deported, and some were rounded up through provocations by the ghetto police. Approximately 800 men were sent to the Vaivara camp in Estonia in the first deportation on August 6, 1943. The Germans tried to prove to the ghetto Jews that it was a deportation to a real labor camp and not to Ponary by allowing them to receive letters from those deported to Estonia, and they even permitted them to join a transport there.

The second deportation on August 24, 1943, consisted of 1,400 people, this time of both men and women together, including the Jews who had come from the province to the ghetto and had not boarded the death trains of the Kovno–Ponary *Aktion*. The third and most difficult deportation began on September 1, 1943, and lasted four days. The brutal searches for deportation candidates were carried out by the ghetto police, who were reinforced by an auxiliary unit of Jewish thugs and members of the underworld. In total, 5,200 men and women were deported to Estonia;[47] more than 10,000 people remained in the ghetto.[48]

Liquidation of the Ghetto: September 5–24, 1943

The brutal deportations to Estonia brought about the physical destruction of the ghetto. Apart from that, the daily work outside the ghetto was halted, and only the activity in the workshops inside the ghetto continued. Just two concentrations of Jews remained outside the ghetto: the Kailis factory for the production of furs on Sheptitzki Street, and the H.K.P. workshop complex for the repairing of military vehicles on Subotch Street. The families of the workers, real or fictive, were transferred there, while about 9,000 Jews remained in the ghetto itself.[49] It was clear to them that the ghetto's days were numbered.

The assassination of the ghetto head, Yakov Gens, by the Gestapo on September 13–14, 1943, was the first incident.[50] A few days later,

47 Einat, *Hayei Yom-Yom*, pp. 319–324.

48 According to Einat, 12,000 people remained in the ghetto; ibid., p. 324.

49 Ibid., p. 337.

50 Balberyshski, *Shtarker fun ayzn*, pp. 474–475; Katcherginski, *Churbn Vilne*, p. 31; Korchak, *Lehavot Ba'efer*, p. 193.

on Saturday, September 18, an *Aktion* began in the ghetto, but it was abruptly canceled, and the detainees were released. The liquidation actually took place at the end of that week, on September 23, 1943, and on the following day. The Jews were concentrated outside the ghetto, and approximately 2,000 working-age men were separated from the others, loaded onto freight trains, and transported to Estonian camps. The rest—women, children, and the elderly—underwent a *Selektion*. Less than 1,700 women were sent to a labor camp near Riga, Latvia; several hundred elderly and sick were taken to Ponary, and the rest, about 4,000 people, were sent to Sobibor.[51]

Section Two: The Writer in Vilna

Ruth Leimenzon was born in Vilna on February 21, 1910, as Ra'isa (Raya).[52] Her parents, David Leimenzon and Leah Bass, married in late 1907 in Vilna, where David worked as an assistant pharmacist.[53] It seems that their marriage did not go well, and they divorced. In 1913, David Leimenzon married Libba Flexer, also an assistant pharmacist.[54] When World War I broke out and as the front approached Vilna in 1915, the couple nonetheless remained in the city, and two weeks after its occupation by the Germans, a daughter, Ida, was born.[55] Thus, from her early childhood years, Ruth grew up in a family with a stepmother and a sister who was five and a half years younger than her. It is no wonder

---

51 Einat, *Hayei Yom-Yom*, p. 343.

52 See her birth record, Lietuvos valstybės istorijos archyvas (LVIA)-728/4/189. The date on the birth record appears according to the Julian calendar: February 8. All the dates mentioned in the following footnotes are according to the Gregorian calendar. Raya, the diminutive form of her formal name Ra'isa, is mentioned on the inside cover of the original diary.

53 According to their marriage record, they married on December 9, 1907. David was thirty years old and Leah was five years younger than him; see LVIA-728/4/155.

54 According to their marriage record, they married on September 16, 1913. David was thirty-six years old and Libba was five years younger than him; see LVIA-728/4/240.

55 According to her birth record, she was born on October 1, 1915; see LVIA-728/4/256. Vilna was occupied by the Germans on Yom Kippur, September 18, 1915.

that she expressed herself in her diary with the words: "I had always felt alienated and lonely among my own."

During Polish rule in Vilna,[56] Ruth lived with her family at 35 Mickiewicz Street in the Lukishki Suburb. She studied at the Polish Jewish coeducational Gymnasium Oświata (Enlightenment).[57] Although her father already held a respectable pharmacy position, the tuition required by the gymnasium for his daughter was higher than his means, and Ruth was forced to leave her studies and begin working. Thanks to her father's connections in the pharmaceutical field, she got a job at a wholesale company for cosmetics and pharmaceuticals owned by a Pole, where she worked until the Soviet era.[58] When the company was presumably nationalized by the Soviets in the end of 1940,[59] Ruth went to work at a post office, apparently on Dominicans Alley in the Old City.

On April 10, 1938, twenty-eight-year-old Ruth married Bezalel (Tzalel) Trakinski. Tzalel was a native of Vilna, a forty-year-old bachelor merchant, almost twelve years older than Ruth.[60] It is possible that because of this age difference, he was a kind of father figure in her eyes. Thus she wrote about him: "He replaced everyone and everything for me. His loving, ever-smiling face would calm me so much. His always calm and easygoing manner, the exact opposite of me, would work wonders on me, like balm. In his presence, I felt good, very good." They lived at 2 Milosierne Street in the Old City, near Ruth's workplace during the Soviet

---

56 On October 9, 1920, several Polish divisions led by General Lucian Żeligowski occupied Vilna, which was in the hands of the Lithuanians. It was annexed to Poland on March 22, 1922.

57 According to applications for passports from the 1920s, dated April 8, 1924, and October 25, 1922; see LCVA-53/12/15382 and LCVA-53/7/356 accordingly.

58 The Soviets took over Lithuania on June 15, 1940 (including Vilna, which they occupied from the Poles on September 18, 1939, gave it to the Lithuanian government on October 28, 1939), and annexed it to USSR on August 3, 1940.

59 The Law of Nationalization of Private Businesses in Soviet Lithuania was enacted on September 27, 1940, and its implementation was set for September 27–29; Yosef Gar, *Azoy iz es geshen in Lite* (Yiddish) (Tel Aviv: Hamenora, 1965), pp. 109–116.

60 See their marriage record, LVIA-1817/1/435. His father, Hirsh Trakinski, married Bunya Rudaminski in 1895, but they divorced two months later, and in 1896 he married Reizel Levin of Paberzhe. Tzalel, their eldest son was born on June 8, 1898, and after that they had at least one more son and two daughters.

era.[61] However, their happy marriage did not last long. Her heart seemed to predict this, as she would later recall when writing her diary in the barn: "I actually used to tell him [Tzalel], several times, that I have this strong foreboding that I had it too good."

A few days after the outbreak of war on June 22, 1941, abductions of Jewish men began from the streets and houses. The Trakinski couple prepared a hiding place in their apartment. On July 13, 1941, a Gestapo man was seen approaching their house. Tzalel saw no point in hiding anymore. He was not allowed to take anything with him and he never returned.

Ruth was left alone. She adapted herself to the situation and applied cold logic to deal with each event. This was the case when they began to register furniture found in Jewish homes. Ruth registered only the table and decided to dismantle the rest of the furniture and keep it in the apartment on the assumption that Tzalel would return. However, seeing that the furniture was being taken from the Jews, she realized that she had to hurry up and sell her furniture before it was also taken. She did this quickly and even sold the registered table, buying a simple one instead at a low price. She used the income from these sales for years. Moreover, she decided that she had to save her other belongings, and the wife of her previous Polish employer agreed to take them to her house in packages that Ruth would pack. Indeed, some of these items were also of help to Ruth later on.

A week after the sale of the furniture and a day after the completion of the transfer of the packages to the Christian woman, Ruth and all the occupants of her yard were evicted from their homes and moved to a nearby place designated as a ghetto, Ghetto II, on September 6, 1941. As more and more Jews were driven to this ghetto, it became increasingly overcrowded. Ruth and her five neighbors managed to find a place to live in the apartment of the Felman family at 13 Yiddishe Street. His wife and three children were taken from this apartment during "The Great Provocation" on August 31, 1941, when the future ghetto streets were "cleansed" of Jews, but he himself survived.[62] He was therefore left

---

61 The distance is about 500 meters.

62 Ruth did not provide any details about who Felman was in her diary, although she later mentioned his name many times and even wrote that he saved her life when he registered

alone in a two-room apartment and kitchen, so there was enough space for Ruth and her neighbors. Apart from them, more Jews moved into the apartment, and in Ruth's room their number reached fourteen, since the ghetto was so densely populated.

Ruth was not passive in the ghetto. She was appointed to be responsible for the yard of the building where she lived, which entailed distributing food to the occupants of her yard, about 400 people, every day. She realized that she had to obtain a work permit to survive. Here, too, she took informed, proactive action, joining a group of women with work permits who worked in pavilions in the north of the city on Kalvaryiske Street, about 2 kilometers from the ghetto. She tried to arrange a work permit for herself with her local employer there and indeed succeeded in obtaining one.

Ruth took advantage of her work in the city to buy groceries in the market near the pavilions. It was strictly forbidden to bring food into the ghetto, so she had to smuggle it in by hiding it on her person. Of course, this was dangerous, and sometimes even life-threatening, so the apprehension was terrible, as she herself described it in her diary: "As we would approach the ghetto gate, our hands and feet would begin to tremble. Are they going to let us back in today, or will they take us away?" However, she and many other ghetto residents considered this to be an existential necessity. She sold some of the smuggled food in the ghetto and brought the rest to share with all the occupants of the apartment, who ate together.[63] This was her life for three and a half weeks in Ghetto II, until the liquidation began. On Yom Kippur, October 1, 1941,

---

her as his wife. Indeed, Ruth used to write in her diary the names of her acquaintances, without explaining who they were, perhaps because, as she wrote: "But I am only writing for myself." It should be noted that she did not even mention the first name of Felman on any occasion, and just mentioned his brother, Yosef, once. It appears that this future "husband" of Ruth was Eliya Felman, who was born in 1901. Eliya Felman actually had a brother, Yosef, who was married to Basya Shneidman; see their 1930 marriage record, LVIA-1817/1/401. Basya's brother was Hirshl Shneidman; see his 1931 marriage record, LVIA-1817/1/405. It is possible that he is the Hirshl Shneidman, who is mentioned in Ruth's diary. Moreover, Eliya Felman married in 1925; see his marriage record, LVIA-1817/1/381. It is therefore possible that he had three children who still lived in the apartment in 1941, as Ruth noted in the diary.

63 Felman, who worked in the city, also smuggled food products into the ghetto.

a first *Aktion* was carried out there, and many of the ghetto inhabitants who were at home and did not work outside the ghetto were evicted by armed Lithuanians. Of the fourteen occupants of the room where Ruth lived, ten were seized.

All those left alive were ordered to return to their jobs. Soon after, however, the work permits of some of the ghetto residents were revoked, and Ruth lost her job. It was clear to her, as to most of the ghetto inhabitants, that the ghetto was about to be liquidated. Quite a few people tried to move to Ghetto I to be saved, but Ruth thought this was not the right step for her to take, and believed that a safer place for her would be outside the ghettos. But where? She took advantage of the fact that Felman's work group, whose members had not been deprived of their work permits, worked near the residence of the wife of her previous Polish employer. Ruth took a risk and joined this group, and when they arrived in the area of the Christian woman's residence, Ruth went to her apartment and asked her to quickly look for a hiding place with her acquaintances. However, the woman's inquiries did not yield any solution, as none of her acquaintances were willing to risk hiding Ruth. As a last resort, she herself offered to shelter Ruth. Ruth continued to take risks and joined Felman's group for a few days to move some of her belongings from the ghetto to the Christian woman's home, and then finally left the ghetto and stayed with her. A week later, on October 21, 1941, while at the Christian's home, she heard that the ghetto, Ghetto II, had been liquidated.

Ruth carefully considered her situation. She thought she could not stay with the Christian woman for long. After some deliberation, she decided to take a risk and move to the "lion's den" in Ghetto I. In her opinion, it was the right time to join the work blocks that were being set up in the ghetto at that time, thus securing a job, which meant life. She described her brave decision in these words: "If any of these people was offered an opportunity to leave the ghetto and hide, each one would surely do it. And I actually came here on my own!...After all, I knew beforehand why I was coming back. So no regrets! Wherever fate leads me!"

At the same time, the registration of the holders of the yellow permits and their families was underway. Felman, as a holder of a yellow permit, registered Ruth as his wife. In doing so, she was saved, since anyone who did not have a yellow permit or was not registered on one was taken from the ghetto. Ruth was well aware of the value of this registration, and when it was necessary to register again, she was very careful that another woman would not be registered in her place on Felman's permit.

The surveillance at the ghetto gate intensified, and it became very dangerous to smuggle food into the ghetto. Ruth decided not to risk working outside. Felman would smuggle the food and Ruth, who already had a permit of a worker's wife, stayed in the ghetto and prepared meals with the smuggled food in the room, which was occupied by six people. She describes this period of stability in these words: "I had never led such a peaceful kind of life, without a lot of running around." Ruth also adhered to her principles. One day the toilets in the yard broke down. The Judenrat imposed a fine on every family in the yard. Ruth refused to pay the fine, even at the cost of sitting in the Jewish prison on Lida Alley.[64]

By September 1943, it was already clear to everyone that the end of the ghetto was approaching. Ruth decided to run away. For a whole week, she attempted to get out and was even caught. She finally succeeded on September 21, 1943, and hid with the Polish employer's wife. The liquidation of the ghetto took place two days later. Ruth stayed with the Christian woman for five days, but since everyone was afraid of the Gestapo's searches for fleeing Jews, she decided to set off to an address of a farmer that she had in her possession. On September 27, 1943, after many hardships and great risks, she met a peasant who was willing to hide her in her barn. Thus a new period in Ruth's life began: the period of living in a barn.

64 Lukishki Prison was in the city outside the ghetto. Lida Prison, the Judenrat prison, was inside the ghetto on Lida Alley.

Section Three: The Writer in the Village of Simanuvka

Ruth arrived in the village of Simanuvka on September 27, 1943, that is, 232 days before she began to write in a diary. The rural woman Shenkievitch agreed to shelter her in a barn near her home, and from then until the long-awaited liberation from German rule, there were only minor changes in Ruth's situation, as described below:

(1) September 27–December 5, 1943: During the first seventy days that Ruth stayed in the barn, she had the opportunity to bathe once every two weeks.

(2) December 5–21, 1943: On a cold day on December 5, when Ruth was very cold, the villagers decided to let her into their house, and she stayed there until December 21. Ruth describes this period in these words: "I consider that to be the best time I've had since I've been in the village." She even managed to bathe once, and then she was asked to move to a stable, this time with another acquaintance of the peasant family, a Jew named Eliash who was also in hiding. This occurred on December 21, 147 days before she began to write in a diary.

(3) December 21–24, 1943: Ruth managed to live in the stable for only two days. On December 22, Ruth and Eliash were discovered, and they were forced to flee to a nearby forest. That day Ruth returned to the barn, but the landlady was afraid to keep her there any longer.

(4) December 24, 1943–March 27, 1944: Ruth moved to a nearby barn that was rented by the villager, and there she stayed for ninety-five days. Twice she was almost discovered in her hiding place. She describes this period as follows: "For now, I can surely consider that period as the worst of all times....If hell exists, there is no need to find a better one." After the villagers used all the straw that was in the rented barn, the landlady told Ruth to return to the first barn.

(5) March 27–May 15, 1944: Ruth had stayed in the barn for fifty days before she obtained a notebook and began to write in her diary. It had been 232 days since she had first arrived in the village of Simanuvka.

(6) May 15–July 19, 1944: Ruth wrote in the diary during this period, which may be divided in two:

— May 15–June 8, 1944: Within three and a half weeks, Ruth recorded in her diary everything that had happened to her in Vilna and in the village, writing in a distinctly associative manner.
— June 22–July 19, 1944: June 22, which marked three years since the German invasion of Lithuania, was an important milestone for Ruth. Henceforth, she almost completely stopped mentioning past events in Vilna and the village, and concentrated on her daily life in the barn and on events in the village.

From time to time, Ruth calculated the time that she had spent in the barn: On May 24, she counted 156 days since she had last bathed in the country woman's house and had returned to the barn; on June 22, she counted 270 days since arriving in the village; and on July 8, 1944, 286 days had passed. By the last day, July 19, she had already stopped counting; It was 297 days since she had arrived in the village—almost ten months.

Section Four: Diary Index

Overview of the Diary Entries

As mentioned, the diary, which begins on May 15, 1944, is written in an associative manner with brief departures from the present moment to events that took place in the village in previous months, or in the ghetto in previous months or years. From June 22, 1944, Ruth begins to write only about the day-to-day events, which she continues to do until her departure from the barn on July 19, 1944.

Because the chronological discontinuity of the diary may make it difficult for readers and researchers interested in specific events in the ghetto or village to find them in the book, the entries are presented below in chronological order with a brief summary, including the past events cited in an associative manner in each. This is followed by a table of the events in chronological order, noting the entry day in which the events are cited.

Summary of the Diary Entries in Chronological Order

May 15, 1944

The writer begins her diary, counting the number of days that she has been in the barn. She recalls her last bath in the farmer's house and then goes back associatively to that period, from the day that she was brought into the farmer's house:

- Ruth refers to the periods of December 5–21, 1943, when she stayed in the farmer's house; December 21–24, 1943, when she temporarily moved to a stable before returning to the barn December 24–March 27, 1944, when she stayed in the rented barn.
- She recalls that the following day, March 28, 1944, after she was almost discovered by the farmer Shenkievitch, she had to go to the forest for one day, to the exact same place where she had arrived for the first time six months earlier, on September 27, 1943, and describes how she got to the forest then.
- She returns to September 21, 1943, when she escaped from the ghetto. The next day she learned about the unrest in the ghetto. She recalls the moments of turmoil and terror on the previous Saturday, September 18, 1943, and the joy that prevailed that day after the *Aktion* had been canceled. However, many did not wait for their end, and whoever could, fled to the H.K.P. or to the Kailis blocks. She mentions these two labor camps and notes, following a recent message from the Christian woman from Vilna, that only Kailis continued to operate and, therefore, it was the only remaining, possible place of refuge. From here she returns associatively to other periods and places of refuge that were familiar to her:

  - The period of the Soviet occupation of Lithuania, where a group of actors from German-occupied Łódź found a refuge.
  - The period after the liquidation of Ghetto II, after October 21, 1941, when many traveled to Belorussia, and some even acquired a forged passport of a Christian or Karaite.

– The days before the Kovno–Ponary *Aktion* period on April 5, 1943, when many wanted to travel to the Kovno ghetto.
– The period of deportations to Estonia from August 6, 1943, when some volunteered to travel to Estonia. Although Felman proposed that she go there too, she preferred not to approach death voluntarily. And here she also mentions others who moved away from death:
    - A small group of young people who left the ghetto to join the partisans.
    - Others who like her chose to hide among the peasants.

May 22, 1944

Exactly eight months before, Ruth had received a note from her friends in the ghetto, whom she was to wait for the next day, but the next day the ghetto was liquidated. She returns associatively to her experiences that took place since her last day in the ghetto:

- Her last day in the ghetto, September 20, 1943.
- Life in hiding with the help of the Christian woman in the city, September 21–25, 1943.
- Her wanderings in the villages, September 25–27, 1943.
- Life in the barn, as of September 27, 1943.

Ruth recalls her last adventurous bath in the communal bathhouse in November 1943; then she describes her bathing in the barn, 156 days after her last bath in the farmer's house in December 1943. She also recounts how difficult it was to convince the landlady to allow her to take more baths, which leads to a discussion of her complex relationship with the woman.

May 28, 1944

The writer reflects on the fate of the Jews in the last three years. She returns associatively to the beginning of the war in Vilna:

- Life in the city under Lithuanian–German rule, June 22–September 6, 1941.
- The move to the ghetto, September 6, 1941.

(Circa) June 8, 1944

Ruth describes the global and local situation, and then resumes the description of the following experiences, which she interrupted in the previous entry:

- Life in Ghetto II until her escape to the Christian woman's home in the city, September 6–circa October 15, 1941.
- Life in hiding at the Christian woman's home, until after the liquidation of Ghetto II, October 15–October 23, 1941.
- Life in Ghetto I until the assassination of the ghetto head, Yakov Gens, October 23, 1941–September 14, 1943.

June 22–July 19, 1944

The writer describes the local events chronologically, without any more associative leaps to previous events.

Events in Chronological Order

Event Date	Entry Date
June 22, 1941–September 6, 1941	May 28, 1944
September 6, 1941	May 28, 1944
September 6, 1941–October 15, 1941	June 8, 1944
October 15–21, 1941	June 8, 1944
October 21, 1941 onwards	May 15, 1944
October 21–23, 1941	June 8, 1944
October 23, 1941–April 5, 1943	June 8, 1944
April 5, 1943	May 15, 1944
April 5, 1943–August 6, 1943	June 8, 1944
August 6, 1943, onwards	May 15, 1944
August 6, 1943–September 14, 1943	June 8, 1944
September 18, 1943	May 15, 1944
September 20, 1943	May 22, 1944
September 21–22, 1943	May 15, 1944
September 21–27, 1943	May 22, 1944
September 27, 1943, onwards	May 15, 1944
September 27, 1943–December 5, 1943	May 22, 1944
December 5–21, 1943	May 15, 1944
December 21–24, 1943	May 15, 1944
December 24, 1943–March 27, 1944	May 15, 1944
March 28, 1944	May 15, 1944

Section Five: The Writer's Approach to the Ghetto Institutions

The writers of the Vilna ghetto diaries and memoirs severely censured the ghetto authorities for their harsh treatment of the Jews of Vilna.[65] Ruth did not deviate from this either and sharply criticized the ghetto institutions of all kinds, but only after analyzing, as objectively as possible, the particular situation, taking into consideration the possibilities before the ghetto authorities, and also examining the consequences of their actions, either positive or negative, and only then rendering her judgement of them.

This is how Ruth praised the order in the ghetto, which she considered to be exemplary. She attributed this achievement to the Judenrat departments, which in fact micromanaged all the activities in the ghetto. She described the bureaucratic structure of the Judenrat, not without sarcasm, in these terms: "There was a different department for every matter: housing department, sanitation department, outdoor sanitation police, electricity department, finance department. In short: departments upon departments. There were directors, deputy directors, secretaries, assistant secretaries, and just 'plain government' people." This inflated apparatus of the Judenrat therefore employed many officials, junior and senior, whose job was to ensure exemplary order and discipline in the ghetto, but at the cost of a stern dictatorial policy, which made life difficult for the ghetto inhabitants. Access to one of these officials could have facilitated and greatly assisted quite a few people, but it was a very formidable task, or in the words of the writer: "They did you a big favor if they even talked to you." Apart from this limited access to the officials, their treatment of the ghetto residents was rude, unsympathetic, and sometimes even very brutal: "Some of them had become so caught up in their power that they had forgotten that they too were Jews and that they also found themselves in the ghetto." Her conclusion is couched

---

65 The exception was Zelig Kalmanovitch, whose diary was published in 1951; see Zelig Kalmanovitch, "A togbuch in Vilner ghetto," (Yiddish) *YIVO Bletter* XXXV (1951), pp. 18–92. Note his unique approach referring to the Oshmene *Selektion*; see ibid., pp. 40–42.

in harsh terms: "If a real Jewish state is ever established, according to the same pattern of the ghetto 'government,' then it will be better that it never exists. It's easier to suffer at the hands of strangers."

The most severely criticized department was the Jewish police. At first, Ruth acknowledged the fact that the police had no choice but to obey the Germans' instructions. She therefore directed her criticism at the way things were done and at the behavior of the police, who could have carried out their actions in a slightly more humane manner, but instead they behaved in a disgusting and often even barbaric manner.

> In a time of such pain, such humiliation, all you saw from them was arrogance and impudence.... Some despicable pipsqueak policeman from a small Lithuanian shtetl, wearing leather gloves, his nose in the air, would give you a push, saying, 'Faster, go faster!' He might also beat you sometimes.

This identification of the policemen with the task assigned to them was very conspicuous, and Ruth felt it quite sharply when she wanted to hand a package to Felman, her "official husband," who was brutally dragged by the Jewish police to be sent to a labor camp in Estonia. The policemen prevented her from doing this act of kindness, so she decided to turn to a German for help. This is her account of the incident: "I went to a German and asked him to let me approach Felman....So the German allowed me to go. Isn't that a laugh? This German turned out to be more sympathetic than the Jews."

Ruth was convinced that even the Germans recognized this eagerness of the policemen to carry out their orders without any mercy: "The Germans relied on the Jewish police, who used to carry it out in an exemplary manner.... They would totally forget that they were also Jews and were themselves in the hands of the Germans." Elaborating further, she decried, "They earned the trust of the Germans to such an extent, that they were even sent into the provincial towns to round up people."[66]

However, apart from the trust that the Germans had in the Jewish police, this was accompanied by ridicule, in her opinion, or as she put it:

---

66 The writer refers here to the roundups conducted by the Jewish police in Vilna County.

> The Germans themselves must be laughing at us. Not only did they not have to bother themselves with us, nor did they have to pay the Lithuanians per head, the way they had done before there was a ghetto, but among the Jews themselves they had loyal collaborators.

And here she touched on a sensitive nerve of the violation of Jewish dignity. She attributed this violation most of all to Yakov Gens, the almighty ruler of the ghetto, to whom and to whose instructions all the departments of the Judenrat, including the Jewish police, were subject. Ruth examined the motives underlying his actions and came to the conclusion that he did not carry out the Germans' instructions because of a desire to save himself, since he had opportunities to do so and did not take advantage of them. Moreover, he refrained from fleeing for his life at the crucial moment when he was invited to the Gestapo, and went there in the clear knowledge that they would kill him. Gens acted, in her opinion, out of a sense of self-respect, for which he was even willing to give up his life for death. At this very point, however, she harshly criticized him. If he was willing to give up his life because of his sense of honor, then why did he not spare the dignity of the ghetto Jews? Or in her language, "why did he force us to defile our own overall honor?"

From this perspective, Ruth reiterated the need for Gens and his police to meet the demands of the Germans. Was it really a necessity? she wondered. Would it not have been more proper to refuse to fulfill the instructions of filling quotas of Jews for various *Aktionen*, and to let the Germans do it themselves? The reason why Gens complied with their demands was his desire to save as many of the ghetto Jews as possible by imposing the task on the Jewish police, so that the murderous Germans and Lithuanians, who knew no bounds, would not carry it out. Ruth challenged this approach. It was clear to her that the failure of the Jewish police to carry out the tasks would have led to a swifter liquidation of the ghetto and, as a result, some of the survivors, including herself, could not have been rescued. However, the price of eliminating a few hundred more survivors would not have changed the very bleak picture in her opinion. On the other hand, at least a little of the Jews' honor would have been salvaged, or in her words: "We would not have been spitting on ourselves." This disregard of the dignity of the Jews by Gens and his police, who gravely violated Jewish honor by carrying out even the Germans' most horrible orders against their own Jewish brothers and sisters had, in her opinion, a severe historical consequence, as she explicitly stated in her diary: "The fact that we were humiliated [by the Germans]—that is an entirely different issue. But we ourselves should not have behaved like that, and in my opinion, that leaves a stain of shame on the history of our ghetto."

Foreword to the Yiddish Edition

by Yisrael Rudnitzki

Vilna was liberated on July 13, 1944.[67] The ghetto ruins survived to see among the liberators a group of Jewish young men and young women, partisans from the nearby forests, the first witnesses of resistance and bravery. Soon thereafter, the surviving remnant—those who had survived in *malinas* (hideouts) and had hidden under tombs—a tiny handful, one out of a thousand, returned to their homes, which were no longer there, in the Vilna that they had once embraced.

Ruth Leimenzon continued to lie in her hideout, in a haystack in a barn, just 20 kilometers from her hometown. There was no place to go. People would look at a live Jew like a wild wonder. How does one begin anew? Her near and dear had shared the fate of the Vilna community. She had seen the road that led to Ponary and so, in August 1943,[68] she escaped from the ghetto at the start of the final liquidation.

When Ruth left the barn, on July 19, 1944,[69] her only possession was a notebook in which she had written her experiences. We know that she returned to Vilna and from there joined the stream of survivors, until, with great effort, she finally reached a safe place. Through the years of wandering from land to land and refugee camps, and later in her new

67 The date is corrected here; in the Yiddish edition, it is mistakenly written as August 13, 1944.

68 This is the date that the diarist used in her diary. She was mistaken, since she escaped from the ghetto in September 1943.

69 According to the last entry of the diary, she intended to leave on July 20.

home in America, she protected her diary as an intimate memory of those tragic days and did not part with it until the end of her life. Not until 1968 was the document brought to Israel: a thick notebook with a red cover,[70] 18.5 x 20.5 centimeters, 135 unnumbered pages,[71] written on both sides and from one edge to the other with an ordinary pencil. The first entry is dated May 15, 1944; the last one, July 19, 1944. She writes retrospectively, from memory, about the past events that were fresh in her mind—three years in the ghetto, the destruction of Vilna, and 231 days in Simanuvka, a village near Niementchin.[72] All of this was incorporated in her account of 66 days, dated from day 232 in the barn until the liberation.

After becoming acquainted with the manuscript, there remained no doubt that we had before us an extraordinary document: the only diary, until now, in Holocaust literature about the Vilna ghetto, written by a woman, an ordinary person, with descriptive notes.[73] Unbiased, spontaneous, and at the same time deeply psychological, it contains facts about the stubborn battle of a lone woman, who challenged her sealed fate. Stubbornness, and maybe even miracles, aided her to triumph over this hell.

There are countless documents about the Vilna ghetto: testimonies, diaries, memoirs, and research publications, which reveal the details of this tragic subject—the German crimes, from the first day of occupation until the Red Army marched in, and the systematic destruction of almost 70,000 people, conceived and carried out by the Nazi murder machine. Ruth does not disclose any new facts, other than the details of her own suffering, which is perhaps similar to but also differs from the horror and pain of millions during the years of the Holocaust.

In order to leave evidence for the day of judgment that would surely come, the good Jewish habit of writing things down was for hundreds of prisoners in ghettos and concentration camps raised to the level of an

---

70 Actually, there are two notebooks, both with orange covers.

71 Actually, there are 137 pages in the diary.

72 Niementchin is 24 kilometers northeast of Vilna.

73 Since then, a second, reconstructed diary by a girl from Vilna was published; see Rolnikaite, *I Must Tell*. About this diary, see Dworzecki, *Yomanei Getto Vilna*, pp. 105–106.

obligation that often involved self-sacrifice, in view of the fact that death was inevitable.

Ruth finds herself under the protection of decent Christians, but outside of the barn, death is still lurking. Only now, when there are prospects of survival, it is necessary to be able to persevere. It is not easy. It is already 232 days like this. She needs someone who is patient, so she can talk, talk without stopping, talk it all out, after all those months, so she "finally got a notebook," which means that it wasn't easy for her to acquire one. "Maybe it will make it easier to push through the days," to talk without stopping in order to persevere! We can understand her guileless statement about not being able to even read what she herself wrote. "I don't think about what to write. I just hack away with whatever comes to mind."

Nevertheless, every word is illuminating, every thought as if measured and weighed, every observation deeply thought through and keenly interpreted. To tell a story like this, one must be adept in the "laws" of creative writing. So the wonder is even greater. Ruth is not a master at writing. On several occasions, she writes in the pages of her diary that her Yiddish is "so poor" that she lacks words, which suggests that Yiddish was not her working language in the last years of the catastrophe. She apparently thought that it would have been easier for her to express herself in another language, but she came out of the ghetto with Yiddish. So the mating of two talents came to her aid: her personal, spiritual maturity that sought release in words and that phenomenon, the Yiddish language, that opened up its treasures for her.

Therefore, what is so remarkable in Ruth's diary are the apt associations, the accurately assembled words, epithets, and aphorisms with which she portrays the ghetto tragedies, and the human shadows around her—those who honorably bore the Jewish faith and those who blackened the Jewish name. With proper modesty she relates her intimate problems during the time in hiding. And the horrific episodes of ghetto life are accompanied by judicious observations: "The women did not rest, they lurked and searched [for their arrested men folk] (but only with their tongues, they had no other means.)" When they propose that she betray her false husband as the price for her life, she thinks, "It would be some military justice to free me and to hand him over." "But he didn't make any effort" she delineates with contempt about someone who had the possibility to get her out of arrest.

She calls the Lithuanians "pleasant *chapunes* [snatchers]," and the Jewish police "diligent workers." Concerning the German threats: "On this point, you could trust them," or "whether the Germans won or lost—they were surely victorious over us." When Jews were signing up for Estonia, she writes, "I, however, had decided not to crawl into that trap." "None of the thousands of those slaughtered, and I have in mind our Vilnaites, ever really thought, until the very last moment, that they would not be rescued." During the most anxious moments, she reflects, "All those whom I had left in the ghetto just two days ago were no longer alive.... And they still say that there is a God!" As if to justify the blasphemous talk, she asserts, "Screaming and complaining like the others had done is something that I'm not capable of doing."

These quotes are not presented here to illustrate picturesque word nuances, which would not be the best commendation of a document about the Holocaust and death. These excerpts from the silent dialogue that the author carries on with herself in the pages of her diary indicate the life-threatening atmosphere in which they were written. The diary seethes with savage power, with the inner strength characteristic of many ghetto prisoners who did not give up, who did not resign themselves until the last minute, and who found, among all the ways that led to death, the one that led to life.

Ruth succeeded. In the diary entry of July 4, 1944, she writes in her notebook: "I only know that I have not yet gotten anything out of life. I consider life to be in my debt in a very big way. I would very much like, at least in the second half of my life, to collect payment for this debt." Several years after the liberation, life began to pay her more generously. However, she did not have enough strength or health to benefit from this bounty. In 1955,[74] after a long illness, Ruth Leimenzon breathed her last breath. She was then only forty years old.[75]

Ruth was not always precise about the accuracy of dates, family names, and facts. Sometimes in the same breath, she tells of tragic events

---

74 The year is corrected here; in the Yiddish edition, 1956 was mistakenly written.

75 This is inaccurate. Ruth was forty-five years old.

that occurred in different times. Details were added in footnotes, based on the recently published works on the Vilna ghetto. Unfortunately, we were not successful in confirming the biographical details of many ghetto inhabitants who are mentioned in the diary, since often only their first names were given.

The original manuscript is is preserved in the collection of the Ghetto Fighter's House in Kibbutz Lohamei HaGeta'ot, Israel.[76]

---

76 The diary is stored in the Ghetto Fighter's House Archives as item no. 2119.

The Diary

Ruth Leimenzon Engles, late 1940s.

[May 15, 1944]

At last, I have gotten a notebook in which to write. I have a pencil. I will try. Maybe it will make it easier to push through the days.[1] It's hard for me. As soon as dawn breaks, my first thought is: how does one endure until the end of the day?[2] It feels as if I am trying to push a boat against the current. By nightfall, I am truly so tired that I feel as if I have done the most strenuous work. I have already been pushing on like this for 232 days.[3] Writing comes easy, expressing myself is also easy, but sitting 232 days in a barn, burrowed in straw, not crawling out of the hole, that is already quite different.

True, my circumstances have improved somewhat. First of all, it's spring—today is May 15, 1944. Until a few days ago, it was still cold. But today, I no longer have to pull the fur jacket from all sides to find a way to arrange it so that the wind won't have an opening through which it can get at me. Secondly, in my current hole, I now have the opportunity to sit up, unlike before, when I could only lie huddled in the shadows. Also, a little sunlight is coming in.

Through a small crack, I see a sliver of the sky, the chickens waddling in the orchard, and the Christians filing back and forth between the house and the barn. All of these are things that I didn't have until now.

There is one thing that I have not yet been able to do—to bathe. For 147 days, I have not washed myself, not even my face.[4] I am able to wash my hands with a little bottle of water, but I sometimes don't have even a little water to do this. The last time that I was able to bathe was when I

---

1 Mendel Balberyshski wrote a similar remark in his Yiddish publication, whose translation in English is: "The main thing, a day was pushed off, no more was wanted." See Balberyshski, *Shtarker fun ayzn*, p. 157.

2 This phrase recalls the verse from Deuteronomy 28:67 in the chapter of "rebuke": "In the morning you will say, 'Would that it were evening.'"

3 At this point, when the diary begins, the writer has been in the barn for 232 days, since she entered it on September 27, 1943.

4 This number indicates that the last time the author bathed was on December 21, 1943, the last day she stayed in the landlady's house.

was in the house of the Christian woman.[5] I consider that to be the best time I've had since I've been in the village.

December 5, 1943, was a cold winter's day. One of my cheeks became swollen from the wind. I caught a really bad chill. The Christians could no longer stand to see how I was freezing, so they took me into the house. They gave me a spot behind the oven. It was as warm as a steam bath. True, I had to sit there for hours at a time, like a clay dummy. It was only when there were no strangers present that I could talk with them, walk around the room, and play with the baby. But I sensed that this was too good to last for very long.

And, indeed, that was how it was.

A young man arrived, an acquaintance of theirs, from Niementchin. I don't even know his last name, only his first name, Eliash. They moved both of us to the stable. And there, right away, the next day, we suffered a calamity. On December 22, two *burlaks*[6] climbed up here and, using matches, started to look around, probably searching for something to steal. When they saw us, they climbed down and created a stir, yelling "*zhidy sidyat*!"[7] We escaped into the forest. There was an uproar. Not far from where we were, people were walking around, back and forth. Dogs were barking nearby. Apparently, they were looking for us. We stood near a tree for a very long time until things quieted down. Having no other alternative, I went back to the same Christians, but this time back to the barn. He went somewhere else. I have no idea what became of him. There are rumors going around that he was murdered. I don't want to believe it. I would very much like to meet him again, but who knows what might still happen to me. This man had gone into hiding the very first day that the Germans had invaded, so of course, he had already suffered a lot.

---

5 This refers to the landlady of Simanuvka. She was the wife of the farmer Yozef Shenkievitch, whose name and address are written on the last page of the diary.

6 Burlaks is a Russian term that refers to persons who, harnessed to a rope (known as *lyamka*), towed barges and other vessels upstream, especially on the rivers of the Volga basin before the twentieth century. Most *burlaks* were poor peasants. The diarist probably used this term figuratively to refer to Russian farm laborers or migrants.

7 In Russian. In English: "Jews are sitting [here]!" The Russian term for Jew used here is derogatory.

My landlady was now afraid to shelter me, not even in the barn. She had rented another barn. She kept several cows there and came to feed them three times a day. The woman who owned the barn was not supposed to know that I was there. And so I stayed there from December 24, 1943, to March 27, 1944, a total of ninety-five days. I don't know what yet awaits me. For now, I can surely consider that period as the worst of all times. Although the winter was a relatively mild one, for me it was the severest of my entire life. If hell exists, there is no need to find a better one. The wind would blow in from all sides. I used whatever I had to cover myself. Even the galoshes and the bottle. I would lay them snugly on my feet and wouldn't move. Not much of a solution! The chill would nip right through me. For the entire ninety-five days, I didn't have even a little bit of hot water, only dry food and a bottle of milk. Often the milk would freeze, so I would warm it up under my fur jacket. There were also times when they couldn't bring me anything to eat. Indeed, on more than one occasion, I lay there hungry or tortured by thirst, always in fear of being discovered. There were several occasions when I truly feared for my life.

One day, a bunch of people came to help the landlady with the threshing. A young Christian boy climbed onto the pile of hay on my side and cried out, "Somebody must be hiding here!" Fortunately, no one paid any attention to him and they called him down. My heart simply stopped. I was able to burrow myself further back toward the wall, leaving an empty space. But the boy wouldn't give up. A little while later, he climbed up again and poked around with a rake but didn't find me. I lay there in a feverish state for the rest of the day, until they left.

Another time, I had crawled out of my hole and was sitting on my side [of the barn], covered up with hay. Again an outsider came to help the landlord. This time he didn't come over to my side, but it still frazzled me. They would not have actually killed me, but they would have driven me out, and that would have created an uproar. In that case, my landlady would not have taken me back. As it was, I was always walking on eggshells around her. She was constantly bringing me news: In such and such a place, the partisans found a Jew, killed him, and beat up the owners; in another place, the Ukrainians had conducted a search. She always had something like that to say.[8] And she would add to these stories that she no longer wished to shelter me, that she had never kept anyone for longer than three months, and what did she get out of it, and what did she need this for. And she would give me a whole song and dance: she would ask Mitya,[9] to find me a place, or she herself would find another place for me, perhaps in a house.

I, however, had set a goal for myself—not to leave her. She is a Christian woman who has always taken in Jews, so she is already used to it and isn't fazed by tales. Besides that, I don't want to be seen in the village, which makes it easier to hide. So I would answer her with my own song and dance: God would repay her for all that she is doing for me. God would protect her from all troubles. God would arrange it so that she would marry off her daughter, giving her much joy and pride—this is her weakness.

Like all Christians, she is fanatically pious. Moreover, several times, partisans have taken clothing, horses, and cows from some of the neighbors in the region. So far, only small things have been taken away from her, so she apparently believes that God is repaying her for helping me. In such cases, I immediately receive a festive meal.

On one occasion, partisans had taken a horse from them and promised to bring it back. Several days passed, and they were already bemoaning its loss. But they [the partisans] did bring it back. She sent me a special meal straightaway. So I would praise her in God's name: As far as I am concerned, I want to stay here, where I have it good, and I am happy, and I couldn't ask for things to be better. I would rather stay with her in a barn than with strangers in a house. This would impress her and, the following morning, she would force a smile and hand me a piece of bread with lard, and an egg—the best proof of how good she is to me.

And so it continued until she used up all the hay. And then again the same old story. She didn't want to take me back to her place. That time I didn't resist. I would leave. However, she then invited me to return to

---

8 Besides Lithuanians, the Germans also used Ukrainians, Latvians, and Estonians for some of their *Aktionen*. In the Children and Elders *Aktion* in the Kovno ghetto on March 28–29, 1944, for example, the Germans employed Ukrainians only.

9 It refers to Mitya (a short form of Dmitri) Shenkievitch, the landlady's son.

her. I was afraid of the trip back to her place, because I wasn't sure that I would be able to find my way back.

In the evening, on March 27, [1944] I sneaked out. My legs were giving way, and my head was spinning, but I arrived safely. But immediately the next morning, something went wrong. The old man wasn't supposed to know that I was there.[10] But he caught me right away. He had brought along the woman from the kolkhoz, who was staying with them,[11] and they confirmed that someone was there. I sat terrified. Not knowing who was there, they too were afraid to approach any closer. The Christian woman arrived and she was a nervous wreck. I calmed her down and assured her that I was going away. I did indeed go away and hid under a tree in the nearby grove. The ground was covered with snow, and a thick snow was still falling. I had no idea where to go. I was unfamiliar with the roads and I didn't know anybody. But I didn't think about it too much. I stationed myself and stood there. A short time later, the Christian woman sent word that I should return that evening. Before nightfall, she even sent me a bottle of hot milk. Apparently, my lectures in the name of God were having an effect.

She is afraid of God. All of them also have compassion for me. I have managed to find favor in their eyes. I have also bribed the youngsters, "*Nye pomazhesh, nye poyedesh*."[12] I also think that my connections with my city Christians have had an impact.[13] They see that intelligent Christians are interested in me and so that raises me a little in their estimation.

Fifty days have already passed since that day.[14] During that time there was another incident. Partisans had killed several Germans in the area, so people were expecting searches to be conducted. Of course, I was to

---

10 This refers to the landlady's husband, Yozef Shenkievitch.

11 A kolkhoz is a collective farm. This probably refers to Russians from the Soviet Union who lived in the Vilna region and had managed to support themselves during the war years.

12 This Russian expression refers to bribery, to greasing the palm. A literal translation is: If you don't grease the wheels, you won't be able to travel.

13 This is a reference to the diarist's former Vilnaite employer and his wife, who are mentioned in more detail further on.

14 The diarist is apparently referring to the day of her return to the original barn, March 27, 1944.

be the first sacrifice. But this time, her son stood up for me.[15] "Leave her alone, where will she go?" By chance, I overheard him. In general, they are all good people, and things have actually worked out quite well for me with them.

Standing there in the grove, I recalled how six months earlier, on August 27, 1943,[16] I was also standing here. I was also unable to sit down at that time, because of a tremendous downpour in this very same grove, even at the very same spot, from early in the morning until late in the evening, as I waited for this very same Christian woman.

I left the ghetto on August 21, 1943.[17] How hard was that for me to pull off! The Jewish police had received an order to make absolutely sure that no one should get out. They had walled up almost all of the *malinas* [hideouts]. For a whole week, I didn't sleep at night, looking for a way to get out. I was on the verge of getting out several times, but something would go wrong and I would be blocked. Then a Jewish policeman betrayed me to the ghetto authorities, telling them that I had tried to bribe my way out with offers of money. They arrested me and caused me to suffer a loss. I sat in the police station, totally in despair. I thought that this was the end for me, that I would no longer be able to escape. I was ready to give away everything I had, if only they would let me out. I sensed from all the activity and the tense situation that the ghetto's days were numbered. This was the moment that I had been anticipating from the very first day in the ghetto. I always used to say that politics interested me very little, because whether the Germans won or lost—they were surely victorious over us. They would destroy us completely. Those around me would get angry. This woman, Lutzki, actually got into an argument with me. "Why are you so pessimistic and see everything in black colors?" The fact that they had already killed thousands of people was apparently not enough proof. "No. They need us. This ghetto is of a high level. The Germans continue to praise

15 This probably refers to Mitya Shenkievitch.

16 The date should be September 27, 1943, six months from March 28, 1944.

17 In the Yiddish publication of the diary, the date August 12, 1943, appears, but in the original manuscript, the diarist wrote August 21, 1943. However, she was wrong about this date, as it should be September and not August—it was two days before the liquidation of the ghetto on September 23, 1943.

it. They brought in new machines. All the workshops are in operation. Productive work is being carried out..." I, however, would stick to my opinion and to my plan to remain in the ghetto until the end, and then, at the last moment, I would try to escape. I understood well that being outside the ghetto was also no picnic. The main thing was to wait for the right moment.

Sitting there in the police station, I thought: apparently it is too late. Too bad. One wants so much to survive, but in what way am I any better than the thousands?

Several hours later, they released me. This was the very day that I had made arrangements [with smugglers] once again to get out [of the ghetto].[18] In the evening, a young man led me to a house. There they led me up through a ladder into a store. It had once been Tarshish's haberdashery store, on the corner of the streets of Shpitol and Zavalne.[19] This was the place from which I was supposed to escape. Once again the same thing. I couldn't get out. The streets were full of Lithuanians. We looked out through a small crack for a long time. Impossible! Some Jew had thrown a sack of potatoes into a hole, and the Lithuanians were running around looking for him as if he were the greatest criminal. Again I remained. I decided not to go out but to wait until morning.

At four in the morning, they finally let me out. I went out of the ghetto onto Zavalne Street. It was still dark. Not a soul on the street. No one was permitted outside before five in the morning. My frame of mind can only be understood by someone who has lived through it himself. Going out on an open street, without a high barricade or fence at every step, and yet, at the same time, being prepared to be stopped at any moment, by anybody at all, even the tiniest pipsqueak, which would mean certain death.

I went through Vingry [Street] and up to Great Pohulanke [Street].[20] The gates and the shutters were still closed, so I had to wander around the

18 This occurred on September 20, 1943.

19 This corner was on the western border of Ghetto I.

20 Going northwest on Zavalne, the diarist could reach Great Pohulanke Street. However, she preferred to go through a smaller, parallel street, by turning through Novogrod to Vingry, which also led to Great Pohulanke.

streets. I managed to get into the "Kailis" block.[21] They never admitted outsiders into their block. I bought a piece of bread and sausage and had a bite to eat there. Over the course of the last week, I had become very hungry. At eight in the morning, I went to my Christian woman.[22] While in the ghetto, I had arranged with Shloyme Shkolnich of Buividz,[23] and with the Shneidmans, Eltchik and Rochele,[24] to go together to the country. I was supposed to arrange with some Christian woman, whose name they had passed on to me, to wait for us and take us out of the city. My Christian woman did in fact immediately go there [to the other woman]. The other woman categorically refused, because she was afraid. But mine promised that she would provide me with such a person.

Now I had to get word to the ghetto [about the change of plans]. Of course, I was very much afraid to go. But what could I do? I had to go! I knew too well what it meant to be in the ghetto, waiting for news from the city, especially in these uncertain days. So indeed, that same day, in the evening, I went to the ghetto. I approached Yisrolik's window through Politzei Street,[25] planning to push the note in through a hole in the shutter, as we had agreed. But a small group of people stood right next to the window. It seemed like they were watching me. Such a terrible panic came over me that I was unable to toss in the note. I headed back. I walked with a normal gait, not running and not looking around me. But my heart was beating very quickly. It seemed to me that someone was following me the whole way. Barely breathing, I managed to get back to the Christian

---

21 The Kailis (fur in Lithuanian) block refers to two worker compounds outside the ghetto, on Sheptitzki Street, which could be reached from Great Pohulanke Street via Slovatzki Street, where Jews worked in the fur factory (Kailis) and lived together with their families. Altogether, about 1,000 people lived there from October 1941. The block remained in use as a workers' camp even after the liquidation of the Vilna ghetto. It was liquidated on July 2–3, 1944, ten days before the Red Army marched in.

22 This refers to the wife of the writer's former Vilnaite employer.

23 Buividz (Bujwidze in Polish, Buivydžiai in Lithuanian) is a village 17 kilometers east of Niementchin.

24 This refers to the couple Eliya Shneidman (b. 1908, Vilna) and Rochele Ptashnik (b. 1913, Podberzh), who married in Vilna in 1937, according to their marriage record; see LVIA-1817/1/431.

25 Polizeigasse was the name of Konske Street prior to World War I. This street was connected to a courtyard in Rudnitzki Street; Balberyshski, *Shtarker fun ayzn*, p. 270.

woman's house. I burst into tears because of all the agitation. But I still had to pass on that note! So early the next morning, I went back, but this time accompanied by my Christian woman. That is to say, she went ahead of me, and I followed behind her, as if traveling separately.

In the ghetto that morning, there was a strange stillness, as if no one was there behind the enclosing walls. A Jewish policeman stood at the ghetto gate. There were no German guards around.[26] I actually wondered: what was the meaning of this deathlike stillness? I pointed the window out to my Christian woman. She pushed in the note and waited on the street for an answer. I didn't want to be hanging around, so I went back to her house. She brought me the reply. They wrote me that things were not calm in the ghetto that day. No one knew exactly what was going on. It was Wednesday, August 22, 1943.[27] It was similar to that last Shabbat.[28]

Yes, I remember that last Shabbat well. I lived through it together with everybody else, lying hidden atop the oven, high up near the ceiling. People believed that this was it, the final liquidation, and that everyone would be taken out. That time, however, it ended up being just an alarm. The Germans put on a show to satisfy their sadistic urges. They stationed a dense guard of armored Latvians around the ghetto. Several trucks drove into the ghetto. Men were captured and packed into the trucks. Our pleasant boss, Kittel himself,[29] ran around to all the houses searching in various holes. The Jewish police themselves had previously blown up almost all the *malinas*.[30] So there wasn't even any place to hide. The

---

26 The ghetto gate was usually guarded on the outside by a Lithuanian policeman and on the inside by a Jewish policeman; see ibid., p. 429.

27 As before, the writer was wrong about the month. The correct date is September 22, 1943, which was indeed on a Wednesday. According to this correction, she actually left the ghetto on September 21.

28 This refers to Saturday, September 18, 1943. Regarding the occurrences on this Shabbat, see Einat, *Hayei Yom-Yom*, p. 338; Balberyshski, *Shtarker fun ayzn*, p. 477

29 Bruno Kittel (1922–1945) was one of the head executioners in the Vilna ghetto during the final phase of its existence, from the beginning of July 1943; see Kruk, *The Last Days*, pp. 580, 584. For more on Kittel, see Sutzkever, *Vilner ghetto* pp. 139–140; Dworzecki, *Yerushalayim DeLita*, pp. 318–319; Kremerman, *MiVilna*, "*Yerushalayim DeLita*," pp. 123–124.

30 This happened during the *Aktion* of the third transport to Estonia, which began on September 1, 1943, and lasted for four days.

panic was great. It was obvious that if they were taking away the final, small remnant of men, they wouldn't maintain the ghetto for the very last group of surviving women and children. The only thing we didn't know was in what manner this [final *Aktion*] would be carried out. Would they finish us off once and for all on the spot? Each *Aktion* had been carried out in a different manner.

They released all the men unexpectedly and told them to go home. The joy was indescribable. People were kissing each other in the streets. But I understood that there was nothing to be happy about. Apparently, when they rounded them up, the Germans saw that, as far as they were concerned, these men were garbage, not labor material. They were elderly men, mostly yeshiva people. It wasn't worth their while to deal with them in any special way. Among this residue of men, a few younger ones had still remained alive and, in general, anybody who had even the slightest opportunity, escaped to the H.K.P. block on Subotch Street,[31] or to Kailis.[32] People gave huge bribes to the Jewish police and also to the Germans to let them out. The story was told that a German had said, "*Die Juden sind dumm*,"[33] that is to say, the ghetto or the H.K.P., it's all the same!

The Jews understood the situation no less than he [the German] did. But when you are struggling against death, you grasp at straws. People thought that maybe we would still manage to be saved. Maybe the blocks [H.K.P. and Kailis] would survive—after all, most of them were craftsmen—in any case, at least gain time. First the ghettos, later the blocks. In the meantime, there might be a tremendous upheaval. None of

---

31 H.K.P., the German abbreviation of Heereskraftfahrpark (Army Motor Vehicle Repair Park), was a complex of vehicle repair workshops that belonged to a German army unit, and employed 350 ghetto Jews. In September 1943, these workers, together with their families, altogether over 800 people, were brought from the Vilna ghetto to blocks of so-called "cheap housing," located in the workshops complex on 37 Subotch Street, east of the area of Ghetto I. Its previous inhabitants of about 1,000 Jews had been massacred prior to the establishment of the ghettos, and the Soviet officers' families who remained in the city were concentrated there immediately thereafter; see Sutzkever, *Vilner ghetto* pp. 160–162. H.K.P. was considered to be a "secure" workplace, and it continued to exist after the liquidation of the ghetto, until it too was liquidated on July 2–3, 1944.

32 The number of Jews there and in H.K.P. after the ghetto liquidation was less than 2,500; see Einat, *Hayei Yom-Yom*, p. 356.

33 In English: "The Jews are stupid."

the thousands of those slaughtered, and I have in mind our Vilnaites, ever really thought, until the very last moment, that they would not be rescued. So they jumped at every which way to escape, but it was all in vain. From the first days, when the Germans came in and I would tell Tzalel[34] to hide from those pleasant *chapunes*, he would answer me that there was no hiding from the Germans. Sooner or later, we are doomed. That's the way it is. Today H.K.P. is also gone.[35] How this actually happened, I don't know, whether they made a *chistke*,[36] or just killed everyone on the spot. Apparently, they can do without craftsmanship, they can manage without our artisans.

I recently received [May 10, 1944] a note from my city Christians.[37] They wrote me that only Kailis remains. And even there, many women and children have died from a typhus epidemic. For me this was significant. When I was working at the post office, during the time of the Soviets (in 1941), I came upon some notes from an actress. Her Yiddish was somewhat more refined than mine, and certainly not with so many errors. I feel ashamed of myself, how poor I am in the language. I simply lack many expressions. But I am only writing for myself. If someone happens to read this, he should not pay any attention to the errors. She wrote in those notes about the experiences of a group of Jewish performers who had escaped from Łódź to Vilna. I was very moved when I read them. We found ourselves in a much worse situation. They still had a place to run to. For us, there was no longer anywhere else to go. We ran from one corner of our cage to the other and squirmed about like captive birds.

---

34 Tzalel Trakinski, the diarist's husband.

35 The diarist was mistaken. The H.K.P. block still existed on May 15, 1944.

36 The diarist uses the Russian term *chistke* (purge, cleansing) to refer to a targeted roundup and killing of specific people, instead of "Aktion," the accepted term in Holocaust literature. This term stems from the time prior to the outbreak of the German–Soviet war, when the NKGB (Soviet secret police and intelligence) ruled in Vilna, arrested alleged "subversive" elements and exiled them to Siberia

37 This refers to her employers before the war.

After the liquidation of the first ghetto (Glezer Street, Yatkever Street, and Gaon Street),[38] an epidemic of traveling to Belorussia broke out.[39] There were no *chistkes* there. That's what people said. Some people forged permits that identified them as Christians or Karaites, so that they could mask their Jewish identities and live outside of the ghetto.[40] Quite a few of them perished this way.[41] Gesya Rabutchin, who had such a permit, thought that she was already on the horse [on her way out]—bye-bye Jewess.[42] She used to stroll along the streets. So she wound up in Lukishki Prison.[43] People who had been there but who had managed to get free saw her there. I myself also had a Karaite permit.[44] I realized however that it was pointless to use it.

A group of over 2,000 men, almost all youths, mostly from the provinces, voluntarily signed up for Kovno.[45] They were promised that

---

38 Ghetto II (the Small Ghetto), the first ghetto that the diarist lived in, since she first moved there from her apartment in the city, was comprised of the streets that she mentions here; she forgot to mention Yiddishe Street, which was one of the main streets of this ghetto and where she herself lived. Almost all of its 10,000 inhabitants were taken to Ponary during the brief period from Yom Kippur, October 1, to October 21, 1941. See Kruk, *The Last Days*, p. 285.

39 According to Balberyshski, with official assistance from the Germans, Jews left for Belorussia, especially to the Lida region before the final liquidation of Ghetto II, and also after the first *Gelbschein-Aktion*; see Balberyshski, *Shtarker fun ayzn*, pp. 226; Kremerman, *MiVilna*, "*Yerushalayim DeLita*," p. 87.

40 The Germans considered the Karaites as non-Jews; see Dworzecki, *Yerushalayim DeLita*, p. 332.

41 According to Dworzecki, hundreds of Jews who had Karaite passes were caught and taken to Ponary; see ibid.

42 This probably refers to Gesya, who was born in 1901 to the Renkatchishek family from Vilna and who was married to Michel Rabutchin, according to their 1923 marriage record; see LVIA-1817/1/196.

43 This refers to the old prison of Vilna, located in the Lukishki suburb, northwest of the Old City.

44 The Karaite Haham (wise man) Seraya Shapshal (1873–1961) prepared a list of his congregation members for the Gestapo, which enabled the Germans to expose the Jews disguised as Karaites; see Kremerman, *MiVilna*, "*Yerushalayim DeLita*," p. 113.

45 These are a few details about the so-called Kovno–Ponary *Aktion* and the murders of April 5, 1943, when about 4,000 Jews from towns of Svientchian, Oshmene, Michalishek, and Svir in the Vilna region were told that they would be taken by train to the Kovno ghetto but were instead transported to Ponary. See Kruk, *The Last Days*, pp. 500–501; Einat, *Hayei Yom-Yom*, p. 315. The diarist refers to the inhabitants of the Vilna ghetto who

they would meet up with their parents and relatives there. Many groups had been transported earlier from one place to the other in peace. So go figure it out! People were always doubtful, but they went anyway! They [the Germans] even made it difficult to sign up—not everyone was accepted. In short, they immediately murdered all of them outside the city so sadistically that a few days later they took people from the ghetto to clean up in Ponary—to cover up the traces.[46] Even their belongings were brought back to the ghetto. Previously, things had been done covertly. Now they put all their cards on the table.[47]

A few weeks prior to the last liquidation, people started to volunteer to be transferred to Estonia and Latvia.[48] Until then, they had remained hidden in their *malinas* just to avoid leaving the ghetto. But they saw that the ghetto was on its way to destruction—it smelled of death. So there was no way out, there was nothing left to lose. Some tried: they need workers there, so maybe they will let us live. That is how they reasoned. Those who had been captured earlier were all killed on the spot. Our neighbors, Mrs. Germaniski, Gurvitch, and Tzipkin, actually left voluntarily. Whether they got there or not, who knows? Many women and children were in the last groups. I even got a letter from Felman.[49]

---

originated in Kovno or to the newcomers from the province, who were also given the opportunity to join those trains; according to Einat, they numbered about 350 Jews. See Einat, *Hayei Yom-Yom*, p. 314. See also Rudashevski, *Yomano Shel Na'ar MiVilna*, p. 103; Balberyshski, *Shtarker fun ayzn*, p. 455.

46 The executions that were carried out on April 5, 1943, lasted an entire day. The next morning 20–30 Jewish policemen from the Vilna ghetto were sent to gather the corpses of those who were shot during an attempt to escape, which lay scattered in the surrounding areas. See Kruk, *The Last Days*, pp. 502–503; Balberyshski, *Shtarker fun ayzn*, pp. 455–456; Rudashevski, *Yomano Shel Na'ar MiVilna*, p. 104.

47 For similar expressions, such as "removed every veil here," see Kruk, *The Last Days*, p. 512; the expression "removed the masks" appears in Balberyshski, *Shtarker fun ayzn*, p. 456.

48 The transfers began on August 6, 1943, when about 800 Jews who were working outside the ghetto were sent to Estonia (Vaivara); Einat, *Hayei Yom-Yom*, p. 319. Other transports followed, as cited later. The transports to Latvia were actually of women, on September 24, 1943, after the liquidation of the Vilna ghetto; see ibid., pp. 342–344; Balberyshski, *Shtarker fun ayzn*, p. 492.

49 Felman is mentioned many times throughout the diary, but without his first name. However, in one of the instances, his brother is mentioned by name, Yosef. Yosef Felman (b. 1902), is probably the son of Tzalka and Rivka Felman of Vilna, who married Basya

He was one of the captured men. I sent him a package. I don't know if he ever received it. We got letters from everyone, but just one time.[50] It is likely that these packages did not find any people alive (I am always pessimistic).

Felman wrote me that they found themselves in a camp and had met those who had arrived there before. He even wrote me that I should come too. I, however, had decided not to crawl into that trap. In those days of traveling, I lay hidden above the oven, because those who walked around openly were being captured.... I reasoned: at least I won't make a fool of myself by going to greet death. If there is already no way out, then death will come on its own.

A small group of youths fled to the forest to join the partisans,[51] and there are probably a few like myself who must be scattered among the peasants, although only a negligible number. For those who now find themselves in German hands, I have little hope. Their program is, after all, not intended only for Vilna. I am far from certain that I will remain alive, but if I do, I would very much like to meet up with as many survivors as possible.

Shneidman, according to their 1930 marriage record; see LVIA-1817/1/401. Yosef Felman had a brother, Eliya Felman (b. 1901), who married Genya Kiesber, according to their 1925 marriage record; see LVIA-1817/1/381. Eliya Felman is probably the frequently mentioned Felman.

50 According to Balberyshski, a batch of letters from Estonia was delivered on August 11, 1943, which conveyed more or less the same message: we are alive, we think we will continue to live, send clothes, especially warm ones, and food. From his further description it may be understood that letters continued to arrive afterwards, prior to the third transport on September 1, 1943; see Balberyshski, *Shtarker fun ayzn*, pp. 469–470.

51 Some groups of members of the Fareinikte Partizaner Organizatziye (United Partisans Organization, FPO), the unified underground organization in the ghetto, which consisted of various parties—Zionist, Communist, and Bundist—that were active in Vilna at the time, escaped from the ghetto into the forest. The second group, which was headed by Yosef Glazman (1908–1943), head of the Lithuanian Beitar from 1938 onward and one of the most active leaders of the FPO, fled on July 24, 1943. See Dworzecki, *Yerushalayim DeLita*, p. 446, 477–479, 499. It is not clear to what extent the diarist was aware of those groups.

[May 22, 1944]

Today is May 22, 1944, exactly eight months since I received the previously mentioned note from the ghetto.[52] They wrote that if the day ends quietly, I should wait for them the following day at the corner of the streets of Zavalne and Shpitol, namely, at the exact same spot from where I had gone out of the ghetto.[53] The next day, August 23, 1943,[54] I went out, accompanied by my Christian woman.[55] From afar, I could see that it was already all over. Many of the windows on Shpitol Street—one could only see those that were near the fence—were wide open. In several houses, the lights were on, not at all blacked out, and one could see that the houses were empty. Still, I approached the designated spot and called out in accordance with the agreed upon signals, but it was in vain; no one answered. On the way back, I encountered a couple with a young girl, escapees. They were looking for a place to spend the night. They had not been allowed into Kailis. I could not get any details from them. They were very nervous. All they told me was that just about everyone had been taken away. That is the last bit of news that I have about the ghetto. I know no more.

Here in the village, there was talk that the Lithuanians and the Germans had spent a long time in the ghetto. They had searched through the malinas and then blew them up. That was indeed likely. Even in my time, if the Germans suspected that there was a hideout somewhere but couldn't find it, they would blow up the entire structure. For that particular task, the Germans relied on the Jewish police, who used to carry it out in an exemplary manner.[56] In this case, I do not

---

52 The diarist received the note on September 22, 1943. This indicates that she was aware that she had left the ghetto in September, and not in August as she previously mistakenly mentioned.

53 The diarist went out of the ghetto on September 21, 1943.

54 Here again, the date is incorrect, it was September and not August.

55 This refers to the Christian woman from Vilna, who is not to be confused with the Christian farmwoman from Simanuvka.

56 The diarist refers to the *Aktion* of the third transport to Estonia, which began on September 1, 1943 and lasted four days, during which the Jewish police blew up almost all of the *malinas*.

hold them [the Jewish police] guilty. I understand quite well that they had to adapt to the situation and follow orders. But, in general, they behaved disgustingly. Their treatment was often barbaric. It's true, I must admit, that order in the ghetto was exemplary,[57] but they could have carried this out in a more humane way. They would totally forget that they were also Jews and were themselves in the hands of the Germans. It would be interesting to know what became of them? How were they thanked for their service?[58]

One can imagine the state of mind I was in when I returned to my Christian woman. Even though I was braced for it, I still cannot comprehend it even today. It was clear. All those whom I had left in the ghetto just two days ago were no longer alive. I had already seen enough facts before this to know that this was the way it was. As I write this, I am reliving it all over again. You want to scream out loud: *Gevald*! So many people, so full of life, with such a will to live! So many small children! And they still say that there is a God!

I recall my last day in the ghetto. The streets were full. Despite all the *chistkes*, people were [physically] still around.[59] They went about idly, grieving and angry. Families who still had some of their members were being torn apart again as people were captured and sent off to Estonia or Latvia. A few had managed to be sent to a transit camp and others had not. So again they had to separate. When people met one another, only one question was heard: Any news? What should we do? The people who were left had no means to escape. They had no *protekzia*,[60] no money for bribery, and were just plain resigned. What can you say when it no longer makes a difference whether you are here or there. There were long lines in

---

57 See, for example, Balberyshski, *Shtarker fun ayzn*, pp. 378–389, 425.

58 The diarist did not know then that the Jewish police had been taken out of the ghetto with the last group during the liquidation and that when they were loaded onto the last wagon trains at noon on September 24, 1943, they were no longer privileged individuals; see ibid., pp. 484–489. Regarding the problematic behavior of the Jewish police, see ibid., pp. 204–205, 221, 278, 423–424; Dworzecki, *Yerushalayim DeLita*, pp. 90–93, 145, 147, 154.

59 The diarist hinted that the mental state of the surviving people was not normal.

60 This Yiddish term means to have influence or pull with people in authority.

the ghetto. You needed a ration card for bread and even for butter.[61] The price of bread in the ghetto was 100 rubles and it was hard to get. Potatoes cost 40 rubles. In general, it was very difficult to get food products. It was no wonder as it had been several weeks since anyone had gone outside of the ghetto. Everyone was excused from their assigned tasks. No one was working. Nothing was being brought into the ghetto, and the majority of people were hungry. In the house, I found the entire Rabinovitch family sitting around, just like people condemned to die, waiting for a pardon. If only someone would throw a bomb, or an earthquake would occur. Let death come already—as long as it is not at their [the Germans'] hands. People were waiting for a miracle. But apparently in our century, miracles do not happen. I told Reeva Rabinovitch that if I managed to get out, I would try to take her with me. She refused. She would not leave her family. Her mother, a religious woman, said that one must rely on God. God will help.

Most of all, I will miss Tzile. Friends like her are rare. Hirshl Shneidman kept going out into the street.[62] He walked from one side of the fence to the other and came back. We greeted him with the same question: Any news? So, go answer!? Sorl went around weeping—Pesach had gone off to H.K.P., and so she got upset over every little thing that happened. We had all been through so much together. So many times we had to run and hide. So many times we thought that the end was at hand. What has become of all of them? They all had believed so strongly in God. Did He help them?

It was impossible to continue staying with my Christian woman.[63] Everyone was expecting the Gestapo to conduct searches.[64] The penalty

61 This refers to cards that the Judenrat's Supply Department issued every month to the ghetto residents; The distribution of food was done according to these cards, which included the right to bread, vegetables, and sometimes other groceries; see, for example, Dworzecki, *Yerushalayim DeLita*, pp. 161–162.

62 This probably refers to Hirshl Shneidman, who was born in 1889 in Smorgon, the son of Ovsey and Chana, according to his 1931 marriage record and to his 1922 passport application; see LVIA-1817/1/405 and LCVA-53/10/3108, respectively. He was apparently the brother of Basya Shneidman (b. 1907), who was married to Yosef Felman.

63 The Christian woman from Vilna and not the Christian peasant in Simanuvka.

64 This refers to searches for Jews in hiding after the liquidation of the ghetto.

for hiding a Jew was death for the whole family. Besides, they often came to look for her son. Lithuanians, in fact, had recently killed him. Before leaving the ghetto, I had gotten an address of a peasant from Buividz, just in case it might be of use. Since I did not know anyone in the village, I decided to go to that address. I made arrangements to be taken there with a certain Christian man to whom my Christian woman had referred me. I myself was unfamiliar with the roads, and I was afraid to ask anyone for directions, since there was no telling whom I might encounter. I decided to travel through the town in a horse-drawn carriage.[65] It seemed to me that would be the safest way.

Shabbat, August 25,[66] in the morning, I settled into the horse-drawn carriage that had been arranged for me and rode off. Two Germans stopped my carriage near Telatnik.[67] I remained sitting there like I was made out of clay. I held my breath. I was sure that they were about to arrest me. It turned out that they were only looking for a ride to the hospital in Antokol.[68] In this way, strangely enough, I traveled with an escort of two Germans! They even tried to start a conversation with me en route. I answered, "*Nye rozumiem*."[69] And that ended that. It was my good fortune that they were not Lithuanians, who would have certainly recognized me as being a Jew. At the end of Pospieshk,[70] I got out and waited for my escort. He was coming toward me riding on a bicycle. I started to approach him [but he rode past without stopping].

---

65 The diarist intended to travel through Vilna in order to reach the person who was supposed to take her to the village.

66 This again is a mistake; it should be September and not August.

67 This refers to a square on the right side of Cathedral Square, at the foot of the Castle Hill. For the possible reasons that explain why this square was called by the strange name *Telyatnik* (*Telyat* means calves in Russian), see Irina Guzenberg, *Vilne: di shpurn fun Yerushalayim deLita* (Yiddish) (Vilna: Pavilniai, 2016), p. 590.

68 Antokol is a suburb in the eastern section of Vilna, along the bank of the Viliya (Neris) River. The way from Telatnik to the military hospital (located between Antokoliye and Sapiezhinske Streets) is circa 4 kilometers.

69 *Nie rozumiem*, in Polish, means I don't understand.

70 Pospieshk, a summer vacation venue, north of Antokol suburb, is located near Oginske Street, along Antokoliye Street and its continuation, Niementchin Street. The distance from the hospital to the end of Pospieshk is less than 3 kilometers.

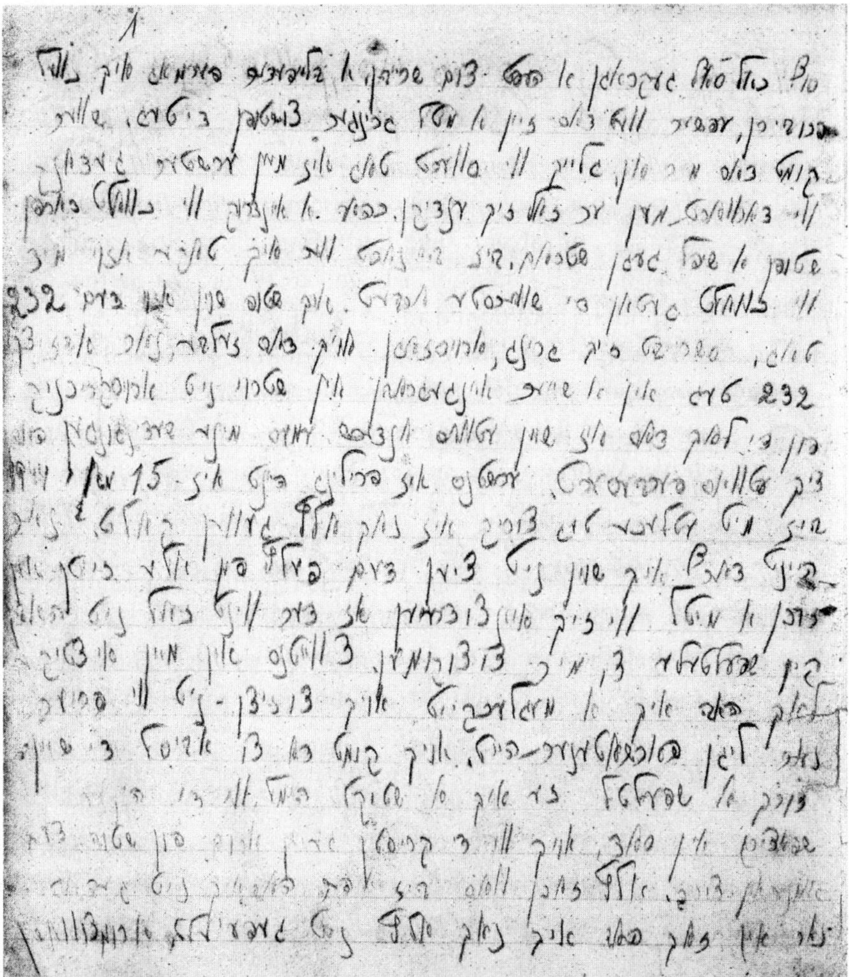

First page of the handwritten manuscript, Collections Section, Ghetto Fighters' House Archive, (GFH), no. 2119.

There was lots of traffic on the road—taxis, trucks full of Germans and Lithuanians, and also a large number of pedestrians—all heading in the direction of the city.[71] I stayed close to the woods. Whenever anyone came near me, I sat down and pretended to be fixing something. After a long time, my escort returned, still riding on the bicycle, heading toward town, but without looking my way. I continued walking. Several hours passed and I had already walked almost 10 kilometers—my man [escort] was nowhere in sight. I began to think that he had gone off to the city and had abandoned me. I sat down and waited. Then I continued on. Finally, I saw him coming from afar. I was so happy, as if I had just seen one of my own relatives. *Nu*, now he would surely tell me how to continue. But it's the same story—he flew by like an arrow shot from a bow! What do I do now? I knew that I was supposed to make a right turn somewhere, but where? I went straight ahead. Maybe he would be waiting for me at the spot where I would have to make the turn. Again, a lot of time passed and I traveled another few kilometers, and still he was not there. I never saw him again. Roaming through the forest, following paths that lead to who knows where, was something that I was afraid to do, so I continued straight ahead until I arrived at Niementchin. This is where I stopped.[72]

Should I go to the shtetl? To whom? I didn't know absolutely anyone there. I climbed a nearby hill and sat down. Should I remain here overnight? A terrible panic gripped me. To be alone in the forest during the day was scary enough, the night was far worse! I crawled down from the top of the hill and remained standing in the middle of the road. The sun had already set. It would soon be dark. I saw two wagons. This time, I didn't hide the way I had before. It was all the same to me now. If they arrested me, so be it, that would be the end.

I was extremely tired and desperately thirsty. My appearance apparently gave me away—it wasn't a cold day, yet I was wrapped in a woolen headscarf and a fur jacket that was not my size. A Christian woman, whom I had visited before my departure, had outfitted me in

---

71 Vilna.

72 The distance to the outskirts of the town of Niementchin via Niementchin Street is about 16 kilometers, which is approximately a four-hour walk.

this way. My despair must surely have been written all over my face. Both wagons stopped—why was I standing here, where was I from, and where did I need to go? I told them that I had run away from the ghetto and was looking for a place where I could at least spend the night. They treated me with compassion. One of the Christians gave me the name of a village and of a family, and told me to go there. For him to go with me to the shtetl was too dangerous, since a policeman might arrest us. He showed me a side road to go down, and afterwards, I still would have to get across a river by boat. It was another 3 kilometers away, so I went further on. After seeing the friendliness of these Christians, I became somewhat bolder. I stopped by a shack and asked for some water. I had become so parched during the day that I barely managed to recover. I also asked them for directions. They even led me to a footpath. Later, a shepherd pointed out a boat. I crossed the river, accompanied by two Christians. Understandably, I was afraid of them. Who knew who they were? Were they from the town? It was already dark and they paid no attention to me.

I went to the riverfront. There was a little village there with small shacks, one very close to the other, full of peasants. They looked at me with curiosity. I called out the family name. It turned out that the whole village had the same surname—they were probably all related—and I didn't know the first name. They asked for a distinguishing mark: what kind of horse did he ride? How should I know! I never paid any attention to that. Apparently, for them, this was one of the most important marks. But none of them had been traveling recently. They pointed toward another shack, somewhat separated from the rest, perhaps that's the place. I went over there and told them openly what I was looking for. They led me into a barn. I settled down into the hay and only then realized how tired I was. The owner, a Christian of about thirty years of age, came in and sat down to amuse himself with me. I told him my whole story and asked if I could stay with him. To my surprise, he began to pour out his heart to me, telling me about all of his bitter life problems: his wife was sick, he didn't live with her, and he needed a woman. Given my state of mind and my general condition, this story was *kak raz*.[73] I pretended not

73 This Russian expression means: a perfect fit.

to understand and tried to steer the conversation to other matters. In this way, he sat [with me] for several hours, until I began to beg him to let me go to sleep. He did me a favor and gave me his place—he slept in the barn—and lay down on the other side with another peasant. I knew that this was not the place for me. With everything else that was happening to me, this was all I needed!

No matter what might happen, I decided that I had to leave this place. With this thought in mind, I fell asleep. In the morning, they brought me something to eat. Again he came to visit with me. I began to entreat him to take me to the village that I was trying to get to. I fed him a story that relatives were waiting for me there and if he didn't accompany me, I would have to muddle along on my own.

Of course, I promised to reward him. It happened to be Sunday, so he didn't have to go to work, and he agreed to do it. He himself was not familiar with the way, but his mother-in-law came from that district, so she told him how to go, more or less. And so we set out. It was a stretch of 20 kilometers, but I had never even thought about how I would manage to get there, being so exhausted from the previous day and also so completely unaccustomed to walking. In the ghetto, such long stretches did not exist.

But I had to do it—and there was no getting around it. He walked ahead and I followed quite a distance behind him.

What a difference between the village peasant and the city clod![74] He treated me with such courtesy. He would look back to make sure that I was coming. He would stop to let me rest. When we passed a well, he would give me a chance to drink and quench my thirst. I remember him with a deep feeling of gratitude. He was especially afraid of crossing train tracks. We made it across. He had to enter a shack and ask for directions several times. He would leave me in the woods and then call out to me. He tried to avoid the roads and travel through the forest, until he got lost and we wound up in a swamp. He managed to get through, but I got stuck deep in mud, up to my knees. The more I tried to get out, the deeper I sunk. Words alone cannot describe what I lived through then. I thought that I

74 This refers to the escort on the bicycle.

was done for, that I would drown. I had saved myself from the ghetto in vain! For the first time in my life, I screamed out such wild cries.

He was already far away from me. But he turned back and dragged me out. Covered with mud, I followed him.

The sun had gone down and he himself was very nervous. At last he came out onto a road. He left me in the woods and went into a shack to get directions. He came out with a peasant girl who agreed to lead us to the village. There were only 2 kilometers left to go. They led me to the very shack that I needed to get to. I stayed in the woods, waiting for it to become totally dark, and then I went in.

The first thing I did was to drink two large ladles of water in one go. The sweeping poverty of the surroundings whistled from every corner. As soon as they heard that I was a Jewess, they actually began to tremble: staying with them was out of the question. It just so happened, that not too long ago, someone had informed on them, and Ukrainians had arrived there looking for Jews.

I was barely able to convince them to let me stay overnight. When I mentioned the person from Buividz, they completely denied knowing her. To this day, I don't understand why she gave me their address. What a reception that was! Despite their poverty, they had no interest in my money. Life is more precious. They made up a bed for me by putting down some hay near the door at the far end of the barn. I threw myself down, not thinking about anything, and fell asleep.

Suddenly it started to pour. The rain dripped down on me from the roof. I curled up in my fur jacket and tried to ignore it. Early in the morning, the Christian woman came in and said that she was going to a nearby village, 3 kilometers away, to dig for potatoes. The Christians that lived there were rich, have a big house, lots of room, and so maybe they would take me in. She knew that Jews have often hidden there. Of course, they were not to know that she was the one who brought me there.

Dead tired, my shoulder and back aching, drenched through and through, I dragged myself after her with what remained of my strength. My brain was no longer working. I could not take stock of the situation that I found myself in. I only knew that I felt like I was walking with someone else's feet. The Christian woman [farmwoman] told me later that she could see from afar what a strain it was for me to walk. She had the impression that I was rushing forward, yet remaining in the same spot. Somehow I got there. My companion went into the field, and I remained on the road.

Several peasant women were already digging potatoes. I didn't know whom to approach and, anyway, there were too many people there. So there I stood, powerless, apathetic, with only one thought in mind—to rest. An older Christian woman wearing a fur jacket, with a kerchief on her head, came toward me. Before I could even say anything, she said to me that she could see who I was, that she would take me in for the night, and that I should go into the woods and wait there until it got dark. For me, it was as if she was sent from heaven.

In my heart, however, I did not feel secure. The day is long and she might yet change her mind. I went into the bushes, leaned up against a tree, and waited there. Sitting down was impossible, because of the previous night's rain. I was happy that at least it wasn't raining during the day. She came back at midday and brought me some baked apples. That was just what I needed. During the last few days that I had been wandering, I had suffered from thirst. I had had absolutely no desire to eat, just to drink. She pointed out her house to me and promised that in the evening she would come to get me.

The day dragged on without end. I dreamed of lying down and stretching out my arms and legs. Every once in a while, I checked to make sure that I could still see the house. God forbid, I should lose sight of it. It started to get dark. It got darker and darker, and I could barely see the house. I became very frightened and set out for the house. At least this way I would be closer to other people. I could hear that they were driving the cattle. I didn't want to go in for fear of ruining everything, so I leaned against a tree near a fence.

It had already grown quite dark when she finally came to get me. She led me into the barn, gave me a piece of bread and butter, and told me to climb up to the top, all the way up near the roof. There I felt happy.

How different things are for me compared to those who remained in the ghetto! That is what I was thinking. Even if they weren't discovered in their hiding places, death by starvation still awaited them. I stretched out my swollen, wounded legs and fell asleep.

The next day, they brought me some pancakes with sour cream, but because I was so exhausted, I couldn't eat for several days. My hostess informed me that as soon as I rested for a few days, they would have to find me a place where I could stay longer.

I told her that I wasn't asking for anything free of charge, that I could pay her, and I begged her to let me stay. [She replied that] She doesn't need any money, she has enough, and she doesn't want to put her family at risk. For me, of course, this answer was distressing. Again I would be wandering from village to village, not knowing which way to turn. In the meantime, since she is letting me stay, I will stay. When they brought me food, I struck up a conversation with the young daughter-in-law and found out that her husband needed a suit.

I latched on to this. It was just my luck that in the next few days he would have to travel to the city. I gave him a note to deliver to my city Christians.[75] He brought back the suit along with several other things. The old woman, it turned out, was not pleased. I had not known that she had been collecting things for her daughter, so I threw in an extra bonus. As a present for her daughter, I gave her a new tablecloth. This really made her happy, and I became a legitimate citizen. For the first three weeks, I sat quietly, asking for nothing. After that, I started to ask them to provide me with the means to bathe. Three weeks had passed without washing myself. They warmed up some water for me and I bathed.

After that, I bathed every two weeks. This wasn't often enough for me at the time, but compared to what was to come later, it was paradise. I also went to the bathhouse several times. My last bath was memorable. It was in November. The Christian woman brought me there and left me alone. I washed myself thoroughly and also washed the little bit of laundry that I had. Suddenly, I heard footsteps. Someone opened the door. I asked, "Who's there?" A male voice replied, "*Przepraszam*!"[76] in a quiet, uncertain voice. He must have been a Jew. Still, I got scared. He probably just wanted to warm himself. I gathered up my belongings, put my laundry in a pail, picked up the bowl and kerosene lantern, and went outside.

---

75 This is a reference to her former employers in Vilna.

76 In Polish, *Przepraszam* means: sorry, or: excuse me.

It was a bright night, but everything suddenly turned dark for me. A blizzard! Everything was covered with snow, and a heavy snow continued to fall. Not a sign of the path. How was I going to find my way back? I stood in the middle of this thick forest and looked all around. I felt frightened and I thought: What should I do? I went back into the bathhouse. I would wait there until the morning. I put everything back, found a place for myself on a board, and was about to extinguish the lantern. What a waste of kerosene. But then I sat up again. No, this was not a good plan. A stranger might come early in the morning and take away the few things that I had. Then I would really be in trouble. The bathhouse was a communal one and was shared by other neighbors. I gathered everything up and went out again. I put down the pail and the lantern, and I pushed the bowl forward through the snow. Then, I went back to get the pail and lantern. And again I pushed the bowl forward. I went on like this for a long time. This way, even if I couldn't find my way to the barn, I would be able to retrace my steps and get back to the bathhouse. But I got really tired and got fed up with the whole thing. So I gathered everything up and began to advance.

My felt boots were full of snow. My knees were wet, even my jacket was wet. I didn't care about anything anymore, as long as I didn't get lost. So that was how I proceeded, with the pail, the bowl, and the burning lantern. Luckily, I did not meet anyone on the way, until I accidentally entered a stranger's yard. The partisans were not yet in control of things at the time as they are today. Again luck was with me: the dog did not bark. Always these miracles. Of course, I made tracks and got out of there as fast as I could.

Somehow, I finally got back. I looked all around at everything. Yes, this was it. This was my "residence." I went into the barn. By the light of the lantern, everything seemed to be peculiar, different, strange. I went out once more. Nevertheless, this was the right place. In the meantime, I spotted fresh footprints. Later on, I caught on that this was under the roof. But, at the time when it was happening, I became frightened that someone was there. I began to search by the light of the lantern. I climbed up the ladder to my hiding place and looked around. I spotted a man's jacket lying there and I yelled out, "Who's there?" although I myself was very scared.

I remembered that earlier that day, the Christian woman had brought the man's jacket. So I climbed back down, put everything back where it was supposed to be, and put out the lantern. In the dark, I groped around for my sleeping spot.

All steamed up from the bath, soaking wet from the snow, and shaken up with fear, this is where I felt the best. I did not take off my wet things but let them dry on me. Because of all the agitation, I couldn't fall sleep. I lay there thinking about my situation. Instead of curling up in a nice warm bed in a heated house after my bath, there I lay, in the middle of winter, in a barn, with the wind blowing in from all sides. And on top of all that, I was thoroughly soaked through and through. But I was happy to at least have this barn. It was much worse for me in the forest.

I never went back to the bathhouse again. I only washed myself one more time, but that was in their house. After that, the issue became entirely irrelevant.

After 156 days, twenty-two weeks, I again washed myself once during the last few days.[77] This caused much excitement. All the women of the house were involved in it. They warmed up a large kettle of water and brought over a long tub, a bowl, and a pail. Everything was carried to the barn. They were afraid to do it in the house in case partisans showed up. I crawled out of my hole, like a drunkard, my legs shaking and my head spinning. To make matters worse, it was a cold windy day. But I didn't want to put it off. I barely managed to reach the water. Everyone came to help me.

I couldn't wait to get into the water. I crawled into that tub full of hot water and washed myself over and over. This was for real, not a dream, as I had often dreamed. Is it possible for a human being who is living in normal circumstances to understand what it's like not to bathe for 156 days? I used to seek ways to make my situation easier to bear. Every day, even on the coldest days, I would take everything off my body, air it out, and sit for a minute totally naked. I would give myself an "air bath." I was

---

77 These words were written on May 22, 1944, which was 156 days after December 19, 1943. Hence the diarist bathed in the landlady's house on this date or prior to it. This date slightly diverges from the date of this bath mentioned on May 15, 1944; then she wrote that she hadn't washed herself for 147 days, i.e., she bathed on December 21, 1943.

waging a battle against the lice. It's not very esthetic to talk about things like this, much less, to write about them. But, for me, this is one of the most important issues. Maybe I'll be able to accustom them gradually to give me at least a bowl of cold water to wash more frequently. For the old woman, this isn't a real necessity. That's why it is so difficult for me to convince her. But lately she has been especially good to me, so eventually I will also achieve this.

My relations with her are always uncertain. They keep on changing. It depends on her mood. For a certain period of time, she did not treat me kindly. She expressed this by reducing my food to a minimum. It got so bad that I would dream about a piece of bread to satisfy my hunger. It was especially bad toward the end of the time when I was still in the other barn, just before I came back here. During the initial period, right after my return, she seemed to forget to bring me food, providing me with just a thin piece of bread and a bottle of milk from morning until evening to sustain me. I don't know what caused this sudden change. I always paid her, both with money and clothing, whatever amount she asked for, never haggling and always in advance.

She, however, always thought that she was cheating herself. At the same time, she didn't want the others in the house, especially her daughter-in-law, to know what she was getting from me. She used to say to me, "They think I am getting rich off of you." She would complain to them that it was actually costing her money, that she was keeping me for practically nothing. Apparently, she wanted to convince them of this and so, by not bringing me food, it was her way of underscoring this point. Be that as it may, I, of course, suffered, but took it all for the good, never complained that I was hungry, thanked them for whatever they gave me, and pretended not to notice, as if this was just the way it was supposed to be.

In response to her excuses, "We couldn't bring it to you," I often wanted to say, "You could have brought me a bigger piece of bread, so I could eat and feel full." But I would control myself and instead answer, "It doesn't matter. If I've managed to last this long, then I won't die from hunger." I would say this in a good-natured way, laughing, until, apparently, her conscience began to bother her. She is also probably afraid that God will punish her. Just then, the old man became ill, and she herself wasn't feeling so well. Besides that, she was worried that something might happen to her daughter, who lives in the city. In a word, she totally changed her behavior. Now, they bring me food on the dot, three times a day, and enough to eat and be satisfied. Every once in a while, early in the morning, even earlier than usual, to show her friendship, she herself brings me a bowl of cereal. Sometimes, during the day, she even brings me something to eat as a fourth meal. At the same time, she says, in a somewhat embarrassed manner, "The day is long, so one chews from boredom." Then I know already that either she has had a dream or something has happened.

Totally unexpectedly, her daughter-in-law went into the city. For a long time now, they have been afraid to travel. People say that everyone is being searched, and things are tense in the city. For me, this was an extraordinary surprise. She brought me back money and clothing. Interestingly, they treat my clothing as if it was their own property, trying it on to see how it fits. In the letter that I gave her, I strongly praised my landlady and her whole family, raising them to the high heaven. Of course, they read the letter before delivering it, and I achieved my purpose. It made the desired impression. They are also greatly impressed with my city connections, people of a higher standing. This is what I sense...

I had only paid through May 1. So I worked out an agreement with her for an additional three and a half months through mid-August and I paid her in advance. And with that, I wished for her to use it all in good health, that she should have much joy and pride from her daughter, and I thanked her for treating me nicely: "I know that she doesn't need my money, that she has enough of her own, and that she keeps me only out of humanitarian decency"—this is her weakness—"that no matter how much I pay her, it is nothing compared with what she does for me." All in all, that's actually not far from the truth. "Otherwise, she would have just taken my money and kept me on bread and water, and I, despite being hungry, would have simply kept quiet. In my situation, what else could I have done, even with money?" (That was a dig regarding earlier times—she understood it.) "She's not taking advantage [of me] and is taking good care of me, just as if I was her summer guest on vacation. God will surely reward her for this." That is how I preached to her.

After hearing my sermon and having just put money in her hands, she totally melted. That didn't necessarily mean that I was now completely sure of her. Her mood often changes. In truth, I have nothing against her. I am truly a good friend to her and her whole family. I only have one wish: that I can stay here until the end of the war. And that brings up the most painful question, when will that be already?

Eight months ago, when I left the city,[78] everybody thought [that it would be], very soon, by winter. I had proposed to myself two deadlines: New Year's Day, and then an extension immediately, until April, for sure! Both deadlines have now passed, and there's no end in sight. Now I have given up hope and no longer put forth any deadlines. My biggest fear is that it will continue once again into winter. I shudder all over at this thought. I dare not think that far ahead.

[May 28, 1944]

Today is May 28, and I have several summer months before me.

A condemned person knows that he has a specific time to be in prison. He subtracts the time that has already passed and so he knows how much time he has left. For me it is quite different. I am constantly counting. Never before did I keep track of the days so precisely, the dates and the months. Right from the beginning, I started to calculate the number of days remaining until my first deadline. It seemed terrible to me. From August 27 until New Year's Day, three full months.[79] So I used to make it easier on myself, dividing the time into weeks and waiting from one Shabbat to the next. For example, today is Shabbat, May 28, so next Shabbat will be June 4, the following Shabbat, June 11, and the fourth Shabbat, June 18.[80] To this very day, I am still using this system. It's already the ninth month that I am pushing time in this way. Also, every

---

78 The diarist left Vilna on September 25, 1943, about eight months before May 22, 1944, the date of this entry.

79 The diarist is mistaken about the date; September 27 was her first day in the barn, but she is right about the number of months until New Year's Day.

80 The author confused May 28, 1944, as well as the other dates listed here, as being the Sabbath when in fact it was Sunday, the Christian day of worship.

day has a different connotation for me. On Shabbat and Sunday, I have the feeling of having completed some kind of task. I have pushed past a week. On Monday, I start counting all over again the number of days until Shabbat. Tuesday, it's already midweek. Wednesday is already nearer to the coming Shabbat. Thursday and Friday, Shabbat is just around the corner. And then, all over again, from the beginning. Of course, this is ridiculous and I'm being foolish. I still don't know how much time yet remains to be counted. It has all become so tedious for me. But I must not complain, I know that quite well. For even without taking into consideration those who have already perished in the ghetto, I can imagine, that many of our handful of survivors are suffering, struggling with their last bit of strength and without any means of subsistence. Compared to them, I have it very good. And yet, I cannot be content.

Today the Christians celebrate *Zielone Świątki*.[81] The landlady herself brought me a full plate of *putcha*[82] and a piece of liver—they slaughtered a calf yesterday—a piece of bread, a morsel of challah, and a cup of sweet coffee. Of course, I thanked her. She looked strangely into my eyes. Apparently, she noticed that I had been crying. Through the crack, I had seen the youngsters all dressed up as they went off to church. I do not envy them. No, I don't even feel that feeling. I wish them the best. But today my heart is especially heavy. I burrow myself deeper into my hole, which is covered with sheaves of grass, like an animal's lair.

A few days ago, the young woman brought me a book.[83] She was trying to give me something that would lift my spirits. It's dark here, and I can't even read what I myself write. I read a little of the book. It's actually quite appropriate for my situation. It describes people who

81 In Polish, *Zielone Świątki* literally means Green Holidays, which is a festival that is linked with the spring agricultural rites. It is celebrated during the seventh week after Easter, leading to Pentecost.

82 The diarist probably meant *petcha* (jellied calves' feet).

83 The book was *Zwycięzca* (English title: *The Conqueror*), the second volume of the *Trylogia Księżycowa* (*The Lunar Trilogy*) by Polish writer Jerzy Żuławski (1874–1915). This trilogy of science fiction novels was written between the years 1901 and 1911, and the specific second volume was first issued in Warsaw in 1910; for an English translation of the trilogy, see Jerzy Żuławski, *The Lunar Trilogy* (Point Pleasant: Zmok Books, 2020).

find themselves on the moon and who are being tortured by some sort of human-like creature that rules over them. These people believe that hundreds of years ago, one of their elders left for the [planet] Earth. He is supposed to return in the shape of a young man and bring them redemption. Their whole religion is based on this. Their clergy are called *Bracia Wyczekujący.*[84] They do not dwell in houses but rather in wards. They include the words "*Przyjdzie, na pewno przyjdzie*"[85] in all their prayers and greetings. This hope gives them courage and the strength to endure all their suffering. Of course, the whole story is a fantasy. And yet, in spite of myself, I compare it with my own circumstances. I find myself, after all, also in a state of waiting, of hoping. Hope also sustains me. But for me, this is not a fantasy. Whether I live to see it or not, the day will come!

It is, however, hard to wait. Oh, how hard! In the beginning, I used to cry continuously. But I realized that this would not do. I would accomplish nothing in this way. After all that I have been through, such a condition can lead to madness. People told the story about this woman Benski who, upon being taken to Lukishki Prison instead of to the ghetto, instantly went mad. That was not the only such occurrence. It's no wonder. That would be even worse than death. If I have actually managed to save myself, then I must hold myself together. I have to control my nerves and rule over them, not they over me. To a certain degree, I have managed to do this.

On the coldest winter days, shivering from the cold, I would talk to myself like this: I am really cold, freezing cold—despite the felt boots and fur jacket, my feet have frozen—but soon it will be Shabbat again, and another week will have gone by. Maybe next month will be warmer. Winter, after all, does not go on forever; it will end. And the time that has passed will not return. It is, after all, closer to the end, I would tell myself, singing various songs and deluding myself with illusions about the future, promising myself, as a reward, mountains of gold. I tried in every way to distract myself so as to free my thoughts from the harsh reality.

---

84 In Polish, *Bracia Wyczekujący* literally means: waiting brothers.

85 In English: He will come, He will surely come.

From time to time, however, my nerves would fall apart. In the last few days, I find myself in a very upsetting condition. I feel as if a ball of thread is stuck in my throat. The air in the barn is, of course, fresh enough, but it seems to me that I just can't breathe. I want to run away from my hole. All I have to do is just push open the door, and I would be in a thick forest with green meadows. Everything is alive and blossoming. After all, it's summer. It has the scent of freshness and freedom. I want to run through the forest, without being afraid that someone might come up behind me, and for no reason at all, just for the fun of it, shoot a bullet into me. I want to run and scream, to hear my own voice. It seems to me that if I could be alone in the field and scream it all out, my heart would grow lighter (strange wild ideas). I want to walk through the city streets, without a yellow patch, on the sidewalk, not in the gutter, not having to be afraid of any toddler, and not avoiding the police guard at the intersections. I want to examine the ruins, go to Ponary. I too, along with many others, have a part of me there. I want to go wherever I wish to go, not as part of a group and not with a guide. I want freedom. It cries out from within me, from my entire being—freedom! How does one live to see that moment? I know, I give myself an accurate assessment, that freedom will not bring me happiness. It is likely that when it comes I will find myself even more unhappy, broken both physically and spiritually, alone, as on a field of corpses. Corpses peer out from every corner. For the time being, I still have hope. Yes, I must admit that even though common sense indicates otherwise, deep in my heart, I am hopeful. You should believe your mind, but the heart feels more strongly. Who knows, maybe?

I hope, I want to hope, that Tzalel is alive. Maybe he escaped to the Soviets and saved himself? You never know, perhaps he succeeded. However, after everything that has happened to us here, you can't base expectations on what has happened to me. Here I am, having saved myself. For now, I am alive; maybe he also lives! For me, that would be the best reward for all my suffering. I never believed in dreams and I don't believe in them now either. But just a few months ago, I dreamed about him. Several times in a row. And always so clearly, as if it was actually happening. As it is so curiously interesting, I will describe it.

The first time, I am in a house, sitting on a sofa, sewing. People are standing around a table. Who they are, I don't know. The door opens and he comes in. He looks very different; thin, wearing a wig somewhat askew, shaven, in boots, and smiling. I am unable to stand up, so I remain seated. I call out to him, "Tzalel." He answers me, "Yes, Tzalel." He sits down beside me. I ask him again, "Is it really you?" He answers me strangely: "I don't recognize you, and you don't recognize me." He presses me so tightly to him that I wake up...

The second time, the dream takes place in Bernardine Park.[86] It is Shabbat. I arrive in a wagon, bringing blankets for some institution. I am helping to take down the blankets from the wagon and carry them into the building, but along the way they keep falling down. He comes along. He is unshaven, wearing his autumn coat, appearing, for some reason, to be sad. He follows me, picks up the blankets, and hands them to me...

The third time, I am sitting in Lukishki Plaza with some acquaintances. All of a sudden, I see from afar, that he is coming: He looks like his usual self, smiling, with his coat in his hand. A broad white ribbon with an inscription, something like what an usher might have, is attached on the sleeve of his jacket. I call out to my acquaintances: "You know what, my husband has returned." I call him. He doesn't hear me, I run after him...

The fourth time, I approach Berzack to call him. I go to the window. Haimovitch is sitting there eating. I ask: "Where is he?" He answers: "He's washing his hands." I see him. He is not wearing a jacket and he is laughing. He spreads the towel and hangs it on the door. He tells me to come in. I go to the door. It gets stuck and I can't get in. This upsets me so much that I actually begin to scream. Several minutes go by before I realize that I am actually lying in a barn... Then I became frightened that someone heard my screams.

Foolish stories. But each time, I really lived them. I miss him so much. They tore a piece of my life from me. He showed me friendship and devotion, something that no one before had ever given me.

---

86 Bernardine Park is located on the bank of Vilnia River, between Castle Tower Hill and Bernardine Monastery. It was created by Bernardine monks in the fifteenth century, and was reestablished, and opened to the public by the Vilna municipality in 1888.

I had always felt alienated and lonely among my own.[87] He replaced everyone and everything for me. His loving, ever-smiling face would calm me so much. His always calm and easygoing manner, the exact opposite of me, would work wonders on me, like balm. In his presence, I felt good, very good. I actually used to tell him, several times, that I have this strong foreboding that I had it too good. Then he would laugh at me. We were never bored together. Sometimes during the summer, driving out of the city, I wanted to invite someone to join us, but he used to say, it's not necessary, we'll go alone. We were good for each other. And then the Germans came, such a civilized people with such a rich culture, and in a barbaric manner destroyed everything. Just three years ago, we were all still human beings... Who could have anticipated such an imminent disaster.

I can't write. My heart feels like it is being torn apart. My head is splitting. *Gevald*, what has happened in the course of these three years! After all, I have lived through it all. And yet, I myself cannot comprehend it. I write these words with truly bloody tears. Several times, I have had to take a break, put away the notebook, and then resume writing again.

June 22, 1941. It was a Sunday, a beautiful, sunny day. It happened to be my day off. As usual, on such days, we were planning to travel by steamer to Verek.[88] I stubbornly decided that I wanted to straighten out the house first, and this delayed us until 10 A.M. Tzalel wasn't too happy about this. Still, he packed everything that we were to take, and we were just about to leave the house. Suddenly, bombs began to fall, real bombs! Not like during air-raid drills.[89]

We stood there stunned. Everything suddenly became dark for us. From that time on, the sun no longer shone for us. I waited for one of my coworkers to go find out where things stood. They reassured us and told

---

87 It is possibly a hint that the diarist was raised by a stepmother.

88 Verek (Verkiai) is a summer resort north of Vilna near the shores of the Viliya (Neris) River. Many others left that day for Pospieshk and Valakumpe, which were closer; see Dworzetzki, *Yerushalayim DeLita*, p. 22.

89 About planned air-raid drills and real bombs on the first day of war, see ibid.

us to come to work tomorrow. To make matters worse, people were afraid to talk to each other. And the bombs kept falling.

The next morning at 8 A.M., I went to the office, hoping to see someone. Everything was closed. So then I went through Dominicans Alley to the gate. They let me in. I ran up the steps. The door was locked. I knocked. I rang [the doorbell]. Nobody was there. So I ran back. I looked around me. The courtyard was full of people, mostly Lithuanians. There was a sense of unrest in the air. It wasn't until later that I realized the kind of danger I had been in. At the time, they were immediately arresting all Soviet employees.

I tried to telephone the management. No use, all the lines were cut off. A Lithuanian coworker came to me and told me that a friend of hers was due to arrive soon with a car. If I wanted to, I could come along. Of course, I wanted to. I prepared a small bundle for myself. But it was already too late. He didn't come. And so we were caught in the trap.

A rash of decrees, entirely concerning Jews, descended upon us. Jews have to wear an identification badge, a patch with a Star of David on the sleeve. A short time later, an amendment: yellow patches are to be worn on the front and on the back [of their clothing].[90] Jews may not walk on the sidewalk, only in the gutter, and only on the right side. Jews may not walk on the main streets, only through side streets, and only on those which are specifically indicated. Jews may go out only until 6 P.M.[91] Later on, another amendment: only until 3 P.M.[92] They began throwing people out of their residences and taking the men away from the evicted families. The families, together with their bundles, were left in the courtyards. Several days later they were permitted to return to their homes. But the men were not freed.

---

90 There were three stages: first, from July 8, 1941, white patches with a yellow circle with a "J" in the middle; second, on July 15, armbands—blue, according to Dworzetzki, and white, according to Balberyshski—with a Star of David—white, according to Dworzetzki, and yellow, according to Balberyshski; third and last, on August 3, the yellow Star of David. See Dworzetzki, *Yerushalayim DeLita*, p. 27; Balberyshski, *Shtarker fun ayzn*, pp. 127–128.

91 See Dworzetzki, *Yerushalayim DeLita*, p. 29; Sutzkever, *Vilner ghetto*, pp. 14–16.

92 This was issued on September 1, 1941; Kruk, *The Last Days*, p. 84; Sutzkever, *Vilner ghetto*, p. 33.

Men are being snatched off the streets. The guess is that they are probably being taken to [forced] labor. At night they are allowed to return home.[93] Until a raid was conducted throughout the whole city: trucks and cabs suddenly showed up to round up the captives from both the streets and the houses. They searched in all the corners.[94] That was when Tzalel fell into their hands.

For a long time I blamed myself. I should have protected him better. Today I see that it's all in vain. Maybe it's even better this way. They sent them off somewhere. That's what people said. Maybe he was able to save himself. It happened on July 13.[95] That date will forever stick in my memory. I was preparing dinner. He was sitting on the stairs, hidden behind a curtain. He came into the room, calm as always, and started to pack. He took his autumn coat, asked me to give him a loaf of bread and some canned goods, and said to me: "They are coming to take me." I tried to convince him to hide. He replied that it was pointless.

A German came in. Seeing that Tzalel was packing, he was very "friendly" and didn't allow him to take anything, promising that he would bring him back in the evening.[96] He went out without even a jacket, wearing a short-sleeved gym shirt, which was open at the neck, with the autumn coat over his shoulder, wearing summer slippers on his bare feet. He turned around on the steps and left his watch and compass. I was still holding his hand. He pressed my hand so hard it hurt. That was our last goodbye.

I remained alone. Like a madwoman. I just felt like everything had fallen in on me, and I was in the middle of broken fragments. Screaming and complaining like the others had done is something that I'm not

---

93 According to Dworzetzki, the snatchings began on June 27, and not all of the snatched Jews returned to their homes; Dworzetzki, *Yerushalayim DeLita*, p. 26.

94 The same happened in Kovno as well; see Yosef Gar, *Umkum fun der yidisher Kovne* (Yiddish) (Munich: Farband fun Litvishe Jidn in der Amerikaner Zone in Daitchland, 1948), p. 35.

95 Korchak wrote that 2,000 Jews were snatched on that same date; Korchak, *Lehavot Ba'efer*, p. 11. Dworzetzki indicates that this was "the rabbis' day," when the Germans seized rabbis from their homes, according to a prepared list; Dworzetzki, *Yerushalayim DeLita*, p. 31.

96 The Gestapo, who entered houses for the men, ordered them to take just a towel and soup; see ibid., p. 26; Balberyshski, *Shtarker fun ayzn*, p. 140.

Document inspection by the Gestapo at the Rudnitzki Street entrance of the Vilna ghetto, October 24, 1941. Photo Collection, Yad Vashem Archive (YVA), 1044/148.

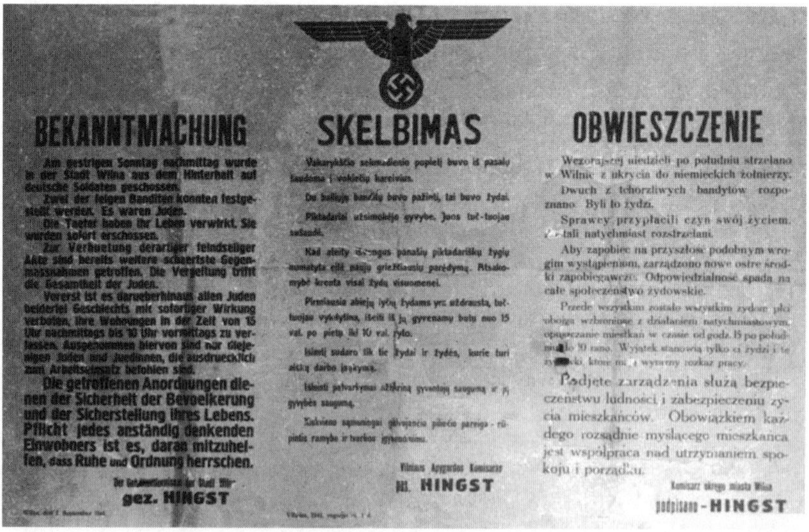

A public notice in German, Lithuanian and Polish, Vilna, 1941.
YVA, Borowicz Collection, 3380/396.

The ghetto prison, at Lida Alley, Vilna. YVA, Borowicz Collection, 3380/596.

A street in ruins in the ghetto, Vilna, postwar. Photo Collection, YVA, 986/14.

capable of doing. I went into my room, heated up some water, and, of all things, started washing his colored laundry. Perhaps I would be able to send him a package. The neighbors, seeing this, thought I had lost my mind.

But that does not happen so quickly. Apparently, the fragile human being is one of the strongest creatures.

In the evening, I sat down on the steps and waited. I was so foolish that for a long time I actually believed that they would free him. I spent many sleepless nights on the steps. I would sit there until late at night. Pesye went to sleep at a neighbor's. Everyone was going to someone else's house. People were fleeing from their own houses. It was dark in every corner. No one could find a place [to hide]. Sooner or later they took away all the men from the courtyard. Hideouts didn't help.

I went into the house and had a good, long, loud cry. The house administrator, a bad-tempered Lithuanian, made immediate announcements every time a man was captured, and he did it with unmasked pleasure. When handing out the bread ration cards, he stressed the fact that men were not to get cards. The cards were marked with the words "For Jews," so that smaller portions of bread would be distributed.

Several days passed and the men had not returned. People began to comfort themselves with the belief that they would be held for a month and then exchanged, letting some go and taking others in their place. In the meantime, they demanded a "contribution": to deliver a specified sum (I no longer remember how much, but it was a colossal amount), and then they would free all the men.[97] Then they took new hostages, some of the most distinguished people in the community.[98] Among them also was Dr. Vygodski.[99] The newly created committees ran around like

97 The demand was issued to the first Judenrat on August 6. The size of the contribution was 5 million rubles; 2 million rubles were to be immediately handed over at on the following morning at 9 A.M. Kruk, *The Last Days*, p. 71.

98 There were Judenrat members among the hostages; Einat, *Hayei Yom-Yom*, p. 89. The diarist calls them "new," since hostages were also taken in the first days of the German occupation; see Dworzetzki, *Yerushalayim DeLita*, pp. 29–30; Balberyshski, *Shtarker fun ayzn*, p. 127.

99 This refers to Ya'akov Vygodski (1856–1941), a doctor, writer, and community activist, former deputy in the Polish Sejm (legislature), and chairman of the Vilna Jewish community. He was arrested on August 24, 1941, and tortured in Lukishki Prison. He

poisoned mice, collecting money, diamonds, fur coats, and other valuable objects for several days in a row.[100] The Germans had warned that if the demanded sum was not handed over by the designated deadline, they would slaughter all the hostages and inflict severe reprisals on the Jewish population.[101] On this point, you could trust them...

They finally turned over the required sum, but the hostages were not freed,[102] nor were the previously captured men released. On the contrary, they continued to take more and more men away. Bands of Lithuanians, *chapunes*, were running rampant all over town.[103] It was said that they got paid 10 rubles per head.[104] So they had a vested interest in catching as many men as they could. They would drag people out of the best hiding places. One time, in the middle of the night, I heard them tearing down our gate with frightful screams. I was overcome with terror. Tzalel was no longer there. You never knew what they were after, whether they were searching for men, to steal, or simply to kill at random. They had the right to do whatever they wanted with us. There was no punishment for murdering Jews. Instinctively, I began to hide things, actually just to move them from one corner to another.

A band of about ten *chapunes* broke into our courtyard. They split up into two groups and entered the houses looking for men. They searched in the attics, in the cellars, and in all the "holes." They cleansed the courtyard of all its men. Only we women remained. In this way, they cleaned out the whole city. They even took children who were only thirteen or fourteen years old.

Is it possible to describe the despair of these mothers? When they say that a person is stronger than iron, it is truly so. The more you endure,

---

died several days later. He was not one of the hostages. See Dworzetzki, *Yerushalayim DeLita*, p. 50; Balberyshski, *Shtarker fun ayzn*, pp. 135, 149.

100 This is a reference to street committees that were spontaneously established to meet the German requirement; Dworzecki, *Yerushalayim DeLita*, p. 43; Kruk, *The Last Days*, p. 71.

101 See Dworzetzki, *Yerushalayim DeLita*, p. 43; Balberyshski, *Shtarker fun ayzn*, p. 135.

102 The Judenrat hostages were all freed; Einat, *Hayei Yom-Yom*, p. 90.

103 Balberyshski, *Shtarker fun ayzn*, pp. 140, 142.

104 Dworzetzki also refers to a reward of 10 rubles; Dworzetzki, *Yerushalayim DeLita*, p. 27; see also Sutzkever, *Vilner ghett*o p. 17.

the more you become hardened. It even got to the point that mothers would walk over the bodies of their own dead children in order to save themselves from Ponary. How sad and frightening that is. One mother related that while running over the body of her own dead child, she saw a little girl still alive among the corpses. She grabbed the child and ran back with her to the ghetto.[105]

There was no news about the men. No one knew where they had been taken. No one could imagine at the time that they would annihilate so many people. My guess is that while they were being taken somewhere for work, a *Selektion* had surely been carried out. There were many among them who were old and sick. The *chapunes* were not picky when catching men. A head is a head.

The women did not rest, they lurked and searched (but only with their tongues, they had no other means...). One of my neighbors kept wandering around. She would run to the Judenrat every day, maybe they had learned something. She would go to her acquaintances, maybe they had heard something. She even went with a Christian acquaintance to a Lithuanian lawyer, maybe he could find out something? We all used to wait for Mrs. Arlyuk to come back soon, and maybe she would bring some news. She would come home worn out and depressed. It was all useless, no clues. One day she brought back news: letters had arrived at the Judenrat. Everyone headed there. In the meantime, at the Judenrat, they rounded up a group of women and dragged them off to [forced] labor. Letters had in fact arrived, but only from those men who had volunteered for peat work in Bezdan, Kena, and Reshe.[106] So the women complained to each

105 For the testimonies of the first witnesses who saved themselves from Ponary and returned to Vilna, see Dworzetzki, *Yerushalayim DeLita*, pp. 53–55; Kruk, *The Last Days*, pp. 90–92.

106 Bezdan (Bezdonys) is a town around 20 kilometers northeast of Vilna and 6 kilometers southeast of Niementchin. During the final period of the ghetto's existence, almost 400 Jews from Vilna were forced to do peat work. On July 9, 1943, the camp was surrounded by German and Lithuanian soldiers, who threw grenades at the buildings and blew them up. Those who tried to run away were shot, and those who remained were burned alive. Kena is a village 25 kilometers east of Vilna. Nearly 200 Jews from Vilna and 70 Jews from Kena worked at a peat camp there. They were annihilated in a ruthless manner on July 8, 1943. Reshe (Riešė) is a village 15 kilometers north of Vilna. Several hundred

other: "If only my husband had had the sense to volunteer." And quite a while later, after several more *chistkes* in the ghetto, those "sages" were also slaughtered, with the exception of the ones who went to Reshe. No matter how clever you tried to be, you remained a fool. Perhaps, after the war, we will be able to determine if anyone outsmarted Hitler…

There was a story going around, already when we were living in the ghetto, that Torenbarg (they even gave his family name)—he was taken away on the same day as Tzalel—was [seen] riding in a truck with a German.[107] He called out to a Jew, asking him to tell his family that he was alive and in a camp with many other Vilnaites. Even if the story is true, it is certainly not true that they are still alive.

They did not neglect the Jews, but kept on providing them with new decrees…

They began to requisition the furniture of the Jews. I still thought that I could wait for Tzalel, and that he would eventually return. So I wanted to keep everything the way he had left it. I began to look for ways to save the furniture. Today I can only laugh at myself. I took apart the cupboard and made a kitchen table out of the bottom part. The top part, I moved to a corner and covered it up. I defaced the armoire to ruin its appearance. I took down the lamp and hid it. The only thing I couldn't figure out was what to do with the table. We had always taken such good care of it that it gleamed like a mirror.

I was able to convince the Lithuanian to requisition only the table and chairs. When I saw that they were taking more and more furniture out of the houses, I actually sold mine, even the requisitioned table. I took a huge risk. Selling anything in a Jewish house was not allowed. I was extremely nervous that day, to the utmost degree, but the day passed without incident. The next day, I ran around looking for a table. I replaced the requisitioned table with an ordinary one. I dragged down two crates from the attic. Dusye, who happened to be with me, helped me. We made

---

Jews from Vilna and other towns worked in the peat camp there, including Hirsch Glick (1922–1944), the author of the Jewish Partisan Hymn. The workers were brought back to the Vilna ghetto after the liquidation of the Bezdan camp.

107 This probably refers to Fishel Torenberg, who was born in Piotrkov, Poland, in 1899, and who married Fanya Gild in Vilna in 1923, according to a passport application; see LCVA-53/11/5682.

some shelves and put all the things from the cupboard on them. I put the clothes from the closet in a big pile. At that time, I was still keeping everything. I understood quite well that as soon as I gave something away, it was no longer mine. So I took a chance, hoping that maybe they would let us stay and there wouldn't be a ghetto. It seemed to me that if they were taking the furniture, this implied that they were going to let us stay where we were. Otherwise, the furniture could have stayed where it was. I was trying to apply logic. But based on their subsequent treatment of us, it was clear that when it came to Jews, logic didn't apply. As compensation for their lost fatherland, a band of Lithuanians, idlers, were given a free hand in having power over the Jews. So they bossed us around and amused themselves with us, taking our furniture, throwing us out of our apartments, then letting us back in, and conducting pogroms from time to time. They carried out a huge pogrom on Novogrod [Street] and murdered many Jews.[108] It went so far, that some people even began to say that it would be better if there were a ghetto. Then things would become quieter because the thugs would not have the right to enter there. Woe to us that there be such an improvement.

A week after selling my furniture, we were confined in the ghetto.[109] One evening, I was returning from my parents' home, which was located in Lukishki.[110] On the way back, an acquaintance warned me that I should not go further, because there was turmoil in the Jewish streets. I didn't stop. I continued along Ignatovske [Street] and

---

108 The pogrom was carried out by armed Germans on July 17, 1941, in the Novogrod suburb, Novogrod Street is the main street there. According to a widespread version of events, the pogrom was carried out because a Jew pushed a German and wounded him, after the latter had brutally removed him from a bread line. Almost 700 Jews were then dragged out of their houses, tortured at Novogrod Market Square on Novogrod Street and then in Lukishki Prison. From there, the road led to Ponary. See Dworzecki, *Yerushalayim DeLita*, pp. 32–34; According to Korchak, 500 Jews were seized; Korchak, *Lehavot Ba'efer*, p. 12.

109 The Vilna ghetto was established on September 6, 1941.

110 This refers to a suburb northwest of the ghetto; Lukishki Prison was located in this suburb. The diarist's parents lived at 35 Mickiewicz Street, according to their passport applications of 1922 and 1924; see LCVA-53/7/356 and LCVA-53/12/15382, respectively. The distance between their home and the diarist's home was 2 kilometers, a walk of almost half an hour.

Dominicans Alley to the corner of Yiddishe Street. The intersection of Glezer Street, Yatkever [Street], and Yiddishe [Street][111] was full of dead drunk Germans and Lithuanians. Miraculously, I somehow broke through them to Gaon Alley, continued on to Shvartzove [Street], and arrived at my place on Milosierne [Street].[112] The next day, the Jews were not allowed to leave their homes at all. Our "good friends," the Christians, who used to come to the Jews to take clothes [supposedly to safeguard], brought us all the news. An acquaintance of Pesye's, a village peasant, came to see her. As he was taking Mischa's clothing, he tried on each item. This really cut to the heart. He also proposed to do me the favor of coming with a wagon and taking everything away. Pesye made a wisecrack that with every bundle she gave away, things became easier for her—a stone fell from her heart. I still held on to my stones...

These "good friends" told us that day that a whole neighborhood of Jews had been led away. There was a story going around that there had been a provocation, that Jews had killed a German.[113] So this was their way of retaliating. From past experience, the Jews anticipated that the men would be taken away, so all the women and children remained in their homes, and the men went into hiding. Only a few men were able to save themselves in this way. They totally cleaned out all of Glezer [Street], Yatkever [Street], Yiddishe [Street], Dominicans Alley, Gaon Alley, and part of German Street.[114] They literally did not spare a single residence.

---

111 This area was intended to be the center of Ghetto II.

112 The diarist lived at 2 Milosierne. From Shvartzove Street, she had to cross Wide Street. The distance from the beginning of Ignatovske Street to her home was about 900 meters, a ten-minute walk.

113 Jews called it "The First Great Provocation." On the pretext that, from a hiding place, Jews had shot at two German soldiers on Glezer Street on August 31, 1941, special detachments surrounded Vilna's historic Jewish Quarter that day and forced out all the Jews from their homes, under a hail of blows, driving them to the pits of Ponary. This incident was reported on September 1, 1941, in a notice issued by the Vilna area commissar, Hingst. See Dworzecki, *Yerushalayim DeLita,* pp. 51–52; Kruk, *The Last Days*, pp. 82–83; Balberyshski, *Shtarker fun ayzn*, pp. 159–161.

114 Outside of the aforementioned streets, parts of other nearby streets were emptied also during the following night; see Balberyshski, *Shtarker fun ayzn*, pp. 161–162. A few days later, all the remaining Jews of Vilna were transferred to these vacated homes, and that is where the two ghettos, Ghetto I and Ghetto II were established. See Dworzecki,

Every single person, without exception, was driven out. They liberated all the houses.[115]

That's when I realized that I was not going to come out ahead. I have to stop being an exception and also give away my things [for safekeeping] before it's too late. In case I need some item, I might be able to get it back, at least. If I leave my things in the house, they will certainly be lost forever. I couldn't imagine back then that all of these people, thousands, had, in fact, all been massacred.[116] The next day, I forced my way through to my Christian woman.[117] The police turned me back twice. One of them even honored me with a blow. I just turned around and went through another street.

The Christian woman didn't even wait to be asked. She sent her servant and one of her servant's friends and, in the space of three days, working from early in the morning until evening time, they dragged my bundles.[118] Moving them [with a cart] would have been even more risky. During the last couple of days [before the ghetto was established], things got harder. The streets were being patrolled. The penalty for hiding Jewish possessions was death! On the fourth day, they [the servant and her friend] were spared [the effort of transporting the bundles]. They [the Jews] were led to the ghetto that day.[119] I caught a glimpse from the balcony and saw on the cobblestone pavement in the middle of the street, hunched shoulders weighed down by the large bundles they carried.

My eyes glazed over. It seemed to me that it was as if this was happening hundreds of years ago, and that I was actually watching it on a movie screen.[120] My mind just couldn't comprehend it all. Was

---

Yerushalayim DeLita, pp. 52; Kruk, *The Last Days*, pp. 81–83, 97–99; Balberyshski, *Shtarker fun ayzn*, pp. 161–162.

115 The term "liberated" is obviously used by the author in a sarcastic manner here.

116 Altogether, about 5,000 Jews were taken to Lukishki Prison and from there to Ponary; Kruk, *The Last Days*, p. 83; Einat, *Hayei Yom-Yom*, p. 93.

117 This is a reference to the wife of the diarist's former employer in Vilna.

118 This took place on September 3–5, 1941.

119 This occurred on September 6, 1941.

120 Rudashevski used a similar expression, whose English translation is: The first sight of the walk to the ghetto is soon revealed to us. A medieval sight; Rudashevski, *Yomano Shel Na'ar MiVilna*, p. 17.

this really happening? Here they were already taking people from 41 Milosierna [Street], and soon they would come to my house, number 2. I was still thinking that maybe, at the last minute, something might happen, some kind of upheaval, and everyone would be freed. Instinctively, I prepared a bundle for myself. It seemed to me that I was packing the absolute minimum, only the most necessary things, but I couldn't even lift it. I threw everything out again and made a smaller bundle. Again the same thing, it wouldn't budge. Several times I lessened the contents until I finally got it to the point where I could somehow drag it.

A bunch of Christians arrived. They grabbed whatever they could get their hands on. I gave a pillow and a blanket to a Christian woman who happened to be standing at the periphery of the group. I wouldn't have been able to drag all that stuff with me anyway. A short time later, when I asked her to give these things back to me, she totally denied that she had them.

An acquaintance of mine, accompanied by her servant, also came. Even though she came for the sake of friendship, I could sense that she thought that I would no longer be needing any of these things. They [the Christians] understood our situation much better than we did. A Christian woman, who had lived among Jews for eighteen years, resided in our courtyard. Her landlady, Mrs. Arlyuk, praised her to the sky as being absolutely honest. So all morning long, until the very moment when the Lithuanians arrived, I hauled my remaining things over to her place, everything, without exception, even the washtub with a net, a bowl, dishes, jams, marmalades. What not?

We had no food [reserves] whatsoever. That was Tzalel's weakness. At the very last minute, when the Lithuanians were already in the courtyard, I dragged a basket over to her [Mrs. Arlyuk's tenant] with about 15 kilograms of granulated sugar, covered with potato peels. I provided her with all sorts of good things. I didn't want to leave anything behind in the house. But my efforts turned out to be totally useless. Later on, when I took the risk of going out of the ghetto without wearing the patches, and went back to visit her, she told me that the Lithuanians had taken it all away. I was only able to salvage a man's suit, and this too, only with the help of my Christian acquaintance.

Nothing happened, nothing unusual transpired, none of the miracles that I was hoping for occurred. The Lithuanians arrived and gave us fifteen minutes to gather ourselves together.[121] Our Lithuanian said, in a very friendly manner, that we shouldn't try to take heavy bundles, since we wouldn't be able to carry them all the way to our destination, and we would just end up leaving them on the road, the way others had had to do. He, as the designated official in our area, would take the articles that were left behind in a wagon and deliver them to us in the ghetto. How very noble of him!

Everyone was already outside in the courtyard with their bundles. All the doors and windows of the houses were open. I was still in the house. I went to my neighbor's apartment, [where] her window offered a better view of what was going on in the courtyard. When I looked around, I didn't see anyone in any of the windows. There was no one in any of the houses. They were already starting to leave, and still no one was bothering me. I could actually stay! I considered the situation. How was this going to turn out. Should I stay here all by myself? What was I going to do with myself? The janitor would inform on me right away. So I ran down the steps and joined the others. The Lithuanians understood that it was not necessary to guard us. We would go on our own. After all, did we have any other alternative?

We walked through the street. I was quite calm, my head held high and proud (it's ludicrous…). At the gates of the courtyards, Christians stood around watching us.[122] I impertinently called out to one of them: "*Taki wadny vidok, tchemu nie sfotografuyesh?*"[123] We only had a short way to go. Through Shvartzove Alley onto Gaon Alley.[124] They were still in the

121 Engelshtern wrote that two military Lithuanians gave his family half an hour for preparations; Engelshtern, *In ghettos un velder*, p. 11.

122 Engelshtern noted that the Christians filled the sidewalks; ibid., p. 12.

123 In Polish, *taki ładny widok, czemu nie sfotografujesz*? means: Such a pretty picture, why don't you take a photograph? Regarding the taunts directed at the Jews by the Poles and Lithuanians, see Dworzecki, *Yerushalayim DeLita*, p. 62.

124 The distance from the diarist's home to Gaon Alley is about 350 meters, a walk of less than 5 minutes. The gate of Ghetto II was at the entrance to Gaon Alley from Shvartzove Street.

process of putting up the ghetto gate.[125] Us they let in, but not everyone had the good fortune to go directly to the ghetto. People from the more distant districts were first dragged to Lukishki Prison. It was impossible to cram everyone into the ghetto in one go. They were in a big hurry. All the Vilna streets were made "*Judenrein*" in one day.[126] Those who were led away to the prison were robbed along the way. Some of them were released and came to the ghetto with absolutely nothing. Many of them were never even brought to the ghetto. They were led straight to Ponary.[127] They were spared so much suffering.

[June 8, 1944]

Today, after six months, the Christian woman brought me a recent newspaper dated May 31, 1944.[128] I could hardly wait to read it. I wanted to find an answer to the question: When will it all end? What a waste of newspaper. It seems, however, that the Germans are not having any success. As I understand it, they are retreating but, apparently with great resistance. They write about everything and everyone, just not about themselves. They tally the losses of England and the Soviets, citing immense numbers. They write that America is uneasy about the huge loan that it has given to the Soviets, that England is giving Stalin a free hand to take over and bolshevize all of Europe. Along with this, they describe

---

125 The diarist was in the group that was concentrated in the smaller ghetto, Ghetto II. About 10,000 Jews were led into this ghetto; see Dworzecki, *Yerushalayim DeLita*, p. 134; Balberyshski, *Shtarker fun ayzn*, p. 184.

126 *Judenrein* is a German word that means clean or cleansed of Jews. The Nazi's goal was to make the world *judenrein*.

127 According to Einat, many were directed to Lukishki Prison, or first to Lida Alley and then to Lukishki Prison; from there, 6,000 Jews were taken to Ponary; Einat, *Hayei Yom-Yom*, pp. 99, 103. Dworzecki mentioned that 200 professionals who were released came to the ghetto; see Dworzecki, *Yerushalayim DeLita*, p. 70. See also Balberyshski, *Shtarker fun ayzn*, p. 186.

128 This refers to the Christian farmwoman in Simanuvka. The entry date is around June 8, 1944, as can be understood from the text that follows. Six months earlier, during the period from December 5–21, 1943, the diarist lived in the home of this woman and could read newspapers there.

the murderous acts of Stalin, likening him to Nero.[129] Half the newspaper is devoted to a description of how the Soviets murdered the Polish population of a certain town. They gathered together all the townspeople in one place, beat and tortured them, and then spilled gasoline on them, and set them on fire. They describe this with great delight, very precisely, with all the gory details. As I read this, it occurred to me that this is surely their system, the one with which they massacred our Jews. I shudder.

I did not find an answer to my question. I see, however, from their grimness, that the Soviets are winning victories. So I feel a bit happier. I just have to continue sitting in the barn, in my lair, and wait patiently. It would be quite a coincidence if on the anniversary, June 22,[130] they were to leave Vilna. That's only two weeks away. But it doesn't look like that's about to happen.

Last night, I actually had a shower in my lair. It's still pouring down on me now. Apparently, there was a great downpour during the night. The water leaked down on me through the sheaves. I laid down fresh straw and positioned myself in such a way that it only dripped down on my head and feet. I caught a cold, but it's not terrible. It's still a lot better than in the winter.

It's so dark here that I'm writing haphazardly. I might not even be able to read what I have written. But that's not important to me. I write just for the sake of writing. It makes the time pass more quickly. At times, it seems to me like I am having a conversation with someone.

I crawled out to walk around the barn a little. Everyone was still asleep. It must have been about 3 A.M. It was already light outside. I was walking very feebly. My legs were trembling and my head was spinning. I barely managed to crawl back. Here is where I feel the best...

Apparently, it has been quiet around here for too long. Today, six partisans slept here. I had quite a bit of company here. If they only knew... The whole time they were here, I had to lie still without moving. The slightest rustle of the straw can be heard immediately. I was even afraid

---

129 It refers to Nero Caesar (37–68), the fifth emperor of Rome, whose cruel personality and reign are assessed very negatively by most Roman historians.

130 This refers to the third anniversary of the German–Soviet war, which began on June 22, 1941.

to breathe. This too I survived and I was able to hold out until they left. They come here quite often, but the owners avoid bringing them into the barn. Apparently, they had no other choice this time. Some of them are in uniform, wearing *shinels*,[131] military headgear, and some sort of armband on their sleeves. Some of them have rifles. They also have horses. They are spreading out all over this region. They hope to set up a Polish state.[132] Those who live around here are not happy with them, because they keep on taking [incomplete sentence].[133]

While pushing through the ghetto gate, we saw a flowing mass of people carrying bundles. The noise was incredibly loud. Children were crying. People were calling to each other loudly, looking for lost bundles. It was total chaos. Just when someone finally managed to put his bundle down on the ground, one of our own good Jews, good guys, helpers, would turn up and disappear with the bundle.[134] All the streets and courtyards were jammed full. People had to push in order to get through, and everyone was pushing and pulling each other. Everyone was trying to find a spot for himself. People were shoving each other, so as to be able to spread out with their bundles on a little corner on the ground. Throughout the day, without letup, until late at night, fresh masses of people continued to flow through. The streets were not clear, not even for a minute.[135] We actually lucked out with our apartment. We, a group of neighbors, moved into Felman's apartment at 13 Yiddishe Street. He was left alone when his wife and three children had been taken away during the provocation.[136]

131 A *shinel* is a long, thick, wool, military coat.

132 This refers to Polish partisans who were virulent antisemites and were linked to the Polish government-in-exile in London.

133 Henceforth, the diarist continues her description of the establishment of the ghetto, which she had interrupted in the preceding pages.

134 Regarding concerns about the help provided by such Jews before entering the ghetto, see Balberyshski, *Shtarker fun ayzn*, p. 175.

135 For more detailed descriptions of the move of the Jews to the ghetto, see Dworzecki, *Yerushalayim DeLita*, pp. 62–68; Balberyshski, *Shtarker fun ayzn*, pp. 167–172.

136 The diarist refers to "The First Great Provocation" on August 31, 1941, after which the Jews of Vilna's historic quarter were forced out from their homes, and were driven to the pits of Ponary.

Two clean rooms and a kitchen. He [Felman] brought out two big beds. We crammed in, all six of us. I didn't have a pillow or a blanket. We managed to work things out among ourselves!

A ghetto administration was formed, a Judenrat.[137] Police were stationed at various positions to maintain order. The population was registered. The occupied areas were [strictly] controlled. Each person was entitled to only 2 meters of space.[138] The bread ration cards that had been issued were distributed. A provisions committee was in charge of handing out produce. There were one or two people in every courtyard on this committee. They would collect the bread and the little bit of produce, which had already been brought to the ghetto in a special place, and would distribute the respective allotment to each person in the courtyard. In our courtyard, I had that function. I had to divide the produce among the residents of our courtyard, almost 400 people. In this way, we became our own bosses. Everyone, both men and women, were required to work, but you had to have a work permit. From time to time, the Germans would order the committee to provide a certain number of workers. The demand for women was much less than for men, so the committee members would send mostly their own relatives. I had always avoided community work as much as possible, so I had no connections among them. I decided to go to a workplace outside the ghetto and arrange to get myself a permit there.

Things were strictly controlled, but I managed to get through. I attached myself to a group of women who were already standing outside the ghetto gate, waiting to go to Porubanek.[139] But the German who came to pick them up began to check the permits. Anyone who didn't have one was honored with blows. Luckily, another group came

---

137 Concerning the composition of the Judenrat in Ghetto II, see Balberishski, *Shtarker fun ayzn*, pp. 194–212; Kruk, *The Last Days*, p. 120.

138 Compare this to the situation in Ghetto I, where according to Dworzecki, at the beginning 0.7–0.8 quadratic meters were assigned for each person; after the *Aktionen*, it was enlarged to 1.5 quadratic meters; Dworzecki, *Yerushalayim DeLita*, pp. 146, 148.

139 The name of a neighboring village, more than 5 kilometers south of the ghetto and more than one hour by foot, or fifteen minutes by truck, where the airport of the city, used by the German military, was located. The name of this village in the district of Vilna today is Kirtimai.

out. I immediately switched over, and in this way, avoided being beat up. They traveled, without a German, to the barracks in Kalvaryiske Street.[140] I went along. When we got to our destination, I went over to the supervisor, a Pole. I had already been informed that he was a bribe taker, and I pleaded with him [to give me a work permit and let me join the work group]. At first, he refused, but then he yielded and promised that he would let me through in a few days. In the meantime, I should just come. So, for several days I struggled to get out [through the ghetto gate]. They would push me back in, and I would push my way out again. Until finally, I got my permit. Now, I was a legal citizen of the ghetto.

The market was directly opposite the barracks. So people would take a chance, remove their patches [the yellow star], and go shopping. I too did not stand aside. At times, a German would appear and would accompany a group of women and wait until they finished shopping. At such times, we would wear our patches. Before returning home, we would go into a corner and begin to hide [produce] anywhere on our person, under or over [our clothing], just as long as we were not carrying anything in our hands or on our shoulders. Up our sleeves, on our sides, on our bellies, around our necks, in our hair; the men, in their hats and in their boots, whatever method you could think of just to avoid detection. All of a sudden, people were "fixed"—their sides and bellies would expand, hunchbacks would appear. In this way, people trudged along the middle of the street over the cobblestone pavement.

One time, while returning home, I stepped away from the group to buy 2 kilograms of potatoes at the market. When I ran back, to catch up with them—they were still quite close—a policeman stopped me and hauled me to the police station.[141] Four women from our group were already there. The policemen were talking to each other, saying that they should let us go. Instead, they detained us for three whole hours, the whole time threatening to take us to Lukishki Prison. They had nothing to do, they were bored, and so they amused themselves with us. The

---

140 The distance from the ghetto gate to Kalvaryiske Street on the north, near the Kalvaryiske Market, was more than 2 kilometers, half an hour by foot.

141 This refers to the Lithuanian police station, and not the Judenrat police station.

older one took a large sheet of paper, wrote up everyone's biography in detail, and gave it to us to sign. While I was signing, I played the fool and asked for the return of my confiscated permit. He replied that I wouldn't need it in Lukishki.

In such critical moments, I feel as if I turn to stone, almost cold-blooded. So I called out to him: "Don't you have even a drop of humanity in you, any feelings? For 2 kilograms of potatoes, you would lead us to our deaths?" I even scared myself with my impudent tone. The others began to tug at my sleeve, telling me to shut up. One [woman] became so hysterical that she shoved her whole fist into her mouth to keep from screaming.

He didn't say a word, he just kept on smiling. All the officers came in, looked us over, and made jokes at our expense. We were sure that it was all over for us already. Completely unexpectedly, they returned our permits and released us. We were truly lucky that time. In many such similar instances, people never returned to the ghetto. It wasn't until I got back home that I cried as was fitting in such an agitated state.

These are the risks that we took both to buy and smuggle things. As we would approach the ghetto gate, our hands and feet would begin to tremble. Are they going to let us back in today, or will they take us away? The Jewish police would bribe the Lithuanians, but it seldom ever helped. Sometimes they would conduct a superficial inspection, confiscating just a few things and letting most of it go through. At other times, they would confiscate everything.

On such days, they would line us up, one behind the other, and frisk everyone, from top to bottom. Heaps of potatoes, beets, carrots, and cabbages—all sorts of good stuff—would then be piled up by the gate outside the ghetto. They would even confiscate wood. People who worked in certain work units were able to get soup, so they would have to pour it out. Jews were supposed to survive solely on their bread rations. We would return to the ghetto empty-handed. But we didn't quit. We continued to buy things and bring them into the ghetto.

Some of the produce that I smuggled in would be sold, the rest I brought home for personal use. We all ate dinner together. One of us, Taybe, would do the cooking. The others would help. Felman and I used to bring produce from the city. We adjusted to ghetto life. That's how it was until Yom Kippur. That day, a few people remained in the ghetto. The majority, fearing the consequences [of skipping work], went to work.

Coming back from work to the gate, we became suspicious of the silence. Nobody was standing at the gate. There was absolutely no one checking. There was one policeman there but he was inside [the ghetto]. We went in. The streets were totally empty. Normally, people would be waiting for those who were returning from work. I looked around: right next to the gate, on the sidewalk, by the gutter, between Yatkever [Street] and Yiddishe Street, a bunch of Lithuanians were sitting with rifles in their hands. The courtyard was completely empty. I stood there for a while, and Taybe came by, wearing a winter coat, in a sweat. I couldn't understand anything she was saying. I ran upstairs to the house. The door was wide open, and the apartment was empty. No one was there. Bundles were strewn all over the floor, everything was overturned. I ran downstairs again and ran into Felman. He told me that some Lithuanians had attacked and rounded up whomever they could grab. Having a work permit didn't even help. My sister-in-law, Tzalel's sister,[142] had left her two little girls at home, one twelve years old, the other five. They took both of them away. She herself had been with me at work. She ran around the courtyard, pulling her hair out, screaming. Screaming? To whom should one scream? To God? He is apparently completely deaf.

We could sense that it was not over yet. They were resting. It was apparently just a lunch break.

Everyone who had gone to work was allowed back in. They didn't bother anybody. It would have been a waste of time. No matter what, they would find us. It's just like a cat that lets a mouse go; she is sure that she will catch it again. Out of fourteen people, only four of us were left. Ten people from our room had been taken away. We hid ourselves in an alcove, which had been set up under the steps. We sat there all night. The Lithuanians did in fact return. We heard them in the courtyard, again rounding up people. They also came into our house and searched in every corner.

---

142 Tzalel had two much younger sisters: Golda, born in 1906, and Ra'isa, born in 1908; see their respective birth records in LVIA-728/4/133 and LVIA-728/4/163. It is not known to which sister the diarist is referring.

Things worked out for us. Early in the morning, we crawled out. It was all over. The Lithuanians were gone. The devastation was enormous. Many people were missing in every house.[143] People ran to the Judenrat, asking them to intervene, to plead. What could they accomplish? Did anybody pay any attention to them? They registered the names of the people who were taken away. There was no lack of writers. There was also plenty of paper.

And so this was how it suddenly became quite roomy. And they didn't forget the other ghetto [Ghetto I].[144] There they did an even better job. They ordered all those who were not artisans—in effect, this meant all those who did not have a yellow permit—to gather together, with their bundles, and to move into our ghetto.[145] From these "volunteers" who gathered together, they took some to Lukishki and from there to Ponary. The rest they brought to us in the ghetto.[146] For us, it was just the opposite. Those of us who possessed yellow permits were ordered to go, together with our families, to the other ghetto.[147] This switchover occurred before Yom Kippur, so those who had come from there were ensnared in the *Aktion*.[148] Of course, the registration of those who had been taken away

143 According to Balberyshski, who was in Ghetto II on October 1, 1941, during the Yom Kippur *Aktion*, three separate groups, 1,500 Jews in total, were led out of this ghetto to their deaths, two during the day and the last one at night; Balberyshski, *Shtarker fun ayzn*, pp. 215–220. According to Dworzecki, who lived in Ghetto I, 1,700 Jews were taken out of Ghetto II in two groups, one during the day and the other at night; Dworzecki, *Yerushalayim DeLita*, p. 136.

144 Here the diarist returns to events that occurred prior to the Yom Kippur *Aktion*.

145 According to the German plan, Ghetto I was intended for craftsmen and other skilled people and their families, while Ghetto II was for unskilled and unemployed people. The diarist describes here the beginning of the implementation of this plan, on September 15, 1941, when unemployed people were taken out of Ghetto I. However, her account is inaccurate, as she meant regular work permits. The yellow permits, which served as life passes for employed people, were issued only in the beginning of October; see Dworzecki *Yerushalayim DeLita*, p. 101.

146 On that September 15, 1941, 3,550 people were taken out of Ghetto I apparently to be transferred to Ghetto II. Only 600 made it. The rest were taken to Lukishki Prison and massacred at Ponary on September 17, 1941; Kruk, *The Last Days*, pp. 112, 114. According to Balberyshski, 2,000 Jews were taken from Ghetto I to their death; Balberyshski, *Shtarker fun ayzn*, pp. 195–196.

147 The diarist was among those who remained in Ghetto II.

148 The diarist does not actually relate what happened during the Yom Kippur *Aktion* in

was pointless. Even holders of the yellow permits could not get out. There were indeed a few Jews who had connections with the high-ranking Germans. They were able to save a few people from the prison. But this was insignificant compared to the overall number.

On the second day after the *Aktion*, they ordered everyone to go to work, as if nothing had happened. They carried out a new registration of the remaining people. A new normal [life] was established. Woe to us for such normality.

Storm troopers arrived at the barracks.[149] They beat up the Jews with a vengeance. One day, they beat up everyone in the fifth regiment [work unit] so badly, that the next day no one showed up [to work]. So they came to us in the fourth regiment to demand a certain number of workers. We panicked and went into hiding. Still, they took some people. I was also selected to go. By chance, I was standing all the way at the end, and when it came to my row, they already had the required number. So I remained. From time to time, the storm troopers would also beat up our group. I myself managed to avoid getting beat up.

One day they didn't even let us go to work at all. Our so-called work was using brooms to sweep the courtyards, the barracks, and the stalls; washing the windows and the floors; and stoking the ovens. They told everyone to go home. The storm troopers didn't want any Jews in their midst. Our train workers used to tell us that the Germans used to sing, "*Wir wollen nicht, wir brauchen nicht, keine Judenrepublik, keine Judenpolitik*."[150]

Ghetto I. Dworzecki, who lived there, vividly described this *Aktion*; Dworzecki, *Yerushalayim DeLita*, pp. 90–93. See also Rudashevski, *Yomano Shel Na'ar MiVilna*, p. 21; Balberyshski, *Shtarker fun ayzn*, p. 221. According to Kruk, 2,200 Jews were led out on that day; Kruk, *The Last Days*, p. 285.

149 This refers to the barracks on Kalvaryiske Street, where the diarist was working.

150 In English: We don't want, we don't need, no Jewish republic, no Jewish politics. Several songs with similar lyrics were created by the antisemitic *völkisch* movement and they were sung by members of antidemocratic right-wing Freikorps militia during and after the time of the Weimar Republic. The terms *Judenrepublik* and *Judenpolitik* were used to denounce the democratic system of Weimar.

They annulled our permits. We became unemployed. The mood in the ghetto became more and more tense. People spoke more and more about a total liquidation. More and more people moved to the other ghetto.[151] But not everyone who tried managed to do so.

I looked for a way to save myself. I very much did not want to die randomly, in the midst of all this, even though I knew what tortures awaited me. Felman worked in the area where my Christian woman lived. So I went out of the ghetto with his work group, went to her, and asked her to find me a place to hide. She instructed me to come back for her answer. The next day, she told me that none of her acquaintances were willing to take the risk, not for any amount of money. They were too scared. It was indeed very risky. Too bad! So I had to go back to the ghetto and await what fate had in store for me. I didn't dare ask if she herself would take me in. I was just about to leave when she stopped me and told me that I could stay with her. With Felman's help, I went back and forth a few more times, bringing over the few things that I had from the ghetto to her place, and then I alone remained there.

About a week later, the liquidation took place. Sitting in an alcove in the kitchen, near the balcony, I overheard the Christian say to his wife, "*Dzisiaj to już prawdziwe Czerwone Morze*."[152] I had to hold on to something to keep from falling to the ground. He had seen how they were transporting the Jews through Pohulanke [Street] toward Ponary.[153] Even he had been horrified. I asked the Christian woman to go find out if Felman was there. She didn't actually see him, but someone told her that he was still alive. I waited for an opportune moment and then I went to see him. He told me that they had driven everyone out of the ghetto [Ghetto II]. Now only one ghetto remained. Man's nature is such that no matter what is happening around him, as long as he is alive, he seeks to save himself. It was like that with me. I began to think, what do I do with

151 This refers to Ghetto I.

152 In English: "Today it is a real red sea."

153 The distance from the ghetto to Ponary via Trok Street and Pohulanke Street is about 13 kilometers. This transfer occurred on October 21, 1941, and then Ghetto II was liquidated. See Balberyshski, *Shtarker fun ayzn*, pp. 243, 248, 278. The dates cited by Kruk and Dworzecki are inaccurate. See Kruk, *The Last Days*, p. 285; Dworzecki, *Yerushalayim DeLita*, p. 136.

myself? I could only stay with the Christian woman for another week or two, and then what? She even promised to arrange for me to stay at some estate, but the issue would still be the same. If I had to stay there for a long time, they would certainly get tired of it! Go to the ghetto? I had no work and no work permit, which means I was a prime candidate for Ponary. Besides that, even before the liquidation, it was more crowded there [Ghetto I] than in ours [Ghetto II]. So I questioned whether I would even be able to find some corner in the ghetto where I could stay? After all, I didn't have anybody with whom I could stay. Despite this, I decided to try. Perhaps I would manage to set myself up in the ghetto somehow. Also, Felman promised to help me.

I waited until they finished working and went back with the work group. On the way, we met several people who were leaving the ghetto and going into hiding. In the ghetto, things were chaotic. Blocks were being created.[154] People kept moving from one place to another. Nobody knew where things were heading. People were anticipating that something was about to happen. They advised me to turn back, saying, that if I had been out of the ghetto until then, I should certainly not come back when there was such a commotion going on. However, I thought exactly the opposite. Since blocks were being created, maybe I would be able to join one of them. It was exactly the day that I needed to be in the ghetto; later on could be too late. At the same time, I sensed that I was taking a great risk, that I was putting my life on the line. All the way there, I struggled with myself. Maybe I should turn back? But then I imagined what might await me if I didn't set myself up in the ghetto. I would suffer, prevailing upon Christians, fearing every little movement. And then one fine day they would tell me that I had to leave?

With these thoughts in mind, I entered the ghetto. It was already dark. Things were buzzing on Rudnitzki Street. I had already become unaccustomed to the noise, but I was longing to be among Jews. People were pushing and pulling each other with their bundles.[155] Several work

154 Those who worked in specific units, such as, for example, at the railroad, in H.K.P., and so forth, were quartered in separate blocks in the ghetto proper. Jews believed that during an *Aktion*, the unit committees would see to it that "their people" were not led away; Dworzecki, *Yerushalayim DeLita*, p. 147. For a list of blocks, see ibid., p. 149.

155 For a similar description, see Dworzecki, *Yerushalayim DeLita*, p. 147.

units had created blocks in an effort to protect themselves from the *chistkes*. A number of courtyards on Rudnitzki Street and Kamnitzki Street had been assigned to these groups. Anyone who did not belong to these blocks was forced to move out of those apartments and go somewhere else. There was a full-scale relocation going on. Felman's block was on Kamnitzki Street, but it was already so packed there that he couldn't find a spot for himself. I pushed my way to Rudnitzki Street, into courtyard number 11, and positioned myself by the entrance. The courtyard was full of people. Everyone seemed to be upset, waiting for something to happen. I thought to myself, what have I done? It could be that I'm just pushing myself closer to Ponary. If any of these people was offered an opportunity to leave the ghetto and hide, each one would surely do it. And I actually came here on my own! I almost wanted to ask the Christian who had just brought in a wagonload of rationed bread to take me out of the ghetto and back to my Christian woman. But I stopped myself. He might just turn me over to the Lithuanians. After all, I knew beforehand why I was coming back here. So no regrets! Wherever fate leads me!

In the end, it turned out as I had foreseen. Had I not taken a risk that evening, I would have suffered the entire time. But it's all thanks to Felman. If not for him, without a doubt, I would have been marched directly to Ponary the very next day. In such difficult situations, when a person has two options, it is hard to decide what to do. I was standing there extremely agitated. They had already closed the courtyard gate. Felman had joined me. At around 11 P.M., a (Jewish) policeman knocked at the gate and told us to tell everyone that all those who had yellow permits should go to the Judenrat with their families to register. Felman and I went there immediately. He wrote me down as his wife and got me a small blue slip. This was the life pass.[156] People paid thousands for this little slip. We were among the first. Huge lines formed immediately.

156 This occurred at night in the first hours of October 24, 1941, and was referred to by the Jews as "the night of the yellow permits." The holder of a yellow permit could include only three other people under its protection, all of whom were supposed to be members of his family: a spouse and two children up to the age of sixteen. They were issued blue slips, which together with the yellow permit should have served as life passes; Dworzecki, *Yerushalayim DeLita*, pp. 77, 103–105.

Some of the people were carrying small children in their arms who had just awakened from sleep. Those who did not have passes ran around in confusion, trying to get their names added on to someone's life pass. But this was no simple matter. It was terrible to watch parents begging to have their children written down on a pass and in this way to save them at least.[157]

I didn't take one step away from Felman. There was no lack of people who wanted him to write them on his permit. I made sure that no one would trick him out of that little blue slip.

In the morning, they told all the registered individuals to go out, each with his work unit. Germans stood at every gate, rigorously checking every person. Those who appeared to be too old, even people with blue passes, were pushed to the side and were not allowed to leave the ghetto. I was not totally convinced that the Lithuanians were not actually waiting for us by the gate right outside the ghetto to take us away to Lukishki Prison. I even told Felman that if such was the case, we should try to run away. It's easy to talk but then, when the moment comes, it may not be so easy to run.

I was truly astonished when I saw that no one was waiting for us. We went off, unescorted, to his work unit. All the workers and their families stayed there for three days.[158] They allotted us two rooms and we all lay down on the floor, each with his own bundle, like gypsies.

---

157 A similar pandemonium related to the registration also broke out when the Germans issued the yellow permits in the beginning of October. According to Dworzecki, the Germans issued a total of 3,000 permits, so they could protect a total of 12,000 Jews; Dworzecki, *Yerushalayim DeLita*, p. 101. According to Balberyshski, 3,500 permits were issued, hence the protected number of Jews was 14,000; Balberyshski, *Shtarker fun ayzn*, pp. 260, 266. At the time, the ghetto population was about 23,000. This left 9,000–11,000 Jews unprotected and waiting for the next *Aktion*.

158 Kremerman also mentions three days; Kremerman, *MiVilna*, "*Yerushalayim DeLita*," pp. 8–9. Sutzkever mentions several days; Sutzkever, *Vilner ghetto* p. 54. However, other sources mention just a single day for that *Aktion*, and three days for the "second *Aktion* of yellow permits" on November 3–5, 1941; Dworzecki, *Yerushalayim DeLita*, pp. 107–121; Balberyshski, *Shtarker fun ayzn*, pp. 281–284; Rudashevski, *Yomano Shel Na'ar MiVilna*, pp. 23–25; Korchak, *Lehavot Ba'efer*, pp. 37–38, 41–43. Actually, the workers left in the morning and returned in the evening of the next day; Masha Rolnikaite, *Ani Hayevet Lesaper* (Hebrew) (Jerusalem: Ahibar Publishing, 1965), pp. 33–36.

When we returned to the ghetto, we found such devastation! Most of those who were left behind had been taken away.[159] The only ones who remained were those whose *malinas* had not been discovered.

A short time later, they again ordered everyone with yellow permits out of the ghetto and they "cleaned up" once more.[160] That day, as we were leaving the ghetto, we saw a bunch of armed Lithuanians nearby, already waiting to get to work, so as not to lose even one extra moment of time.[161] What we were feeling in our hearts is understandable. I personally did not have any relatives left. I had already been "liberated" from everyone during the very first *chistke*. Still, this had a terrible effect on me. One can imagine how people who were forced to leave behind their relatives felt. There were plenty of such people.

This time only a handful remained.[162] Officially, they did not exist. They were not registered and they were not given bread ration cards. As far as the Germans were concerned, the ghetto consisted only of yellow permit holders and their families. This meant only artisans. As such, they told us, the Vilna ghetto was now all set and no more *chistkes* would take place.

From the Germans, we got a "guarantee"!

They reregistered the yellow permit holders all over again. At the same time, those who remained paid plenty to be registered. There were people who made a big business out of this. Certain units got the right to inscribe parents. The Jewish employees of the Gestapo were among these units. Of course, people seized on this [the possibility of being written in as a parent]. Later on, these Gestapo workers together with their families were gathered up one day and taken away to Lukishki. There, those who

---

159 5,000 Jews were taken to their death on October 24, 1941; Kruk, *The Last Days*, p. 285; Rudashevski, *Yomano Shel Na'ar MiVilna*, p. 25.

160 This began on November 3, 1941, and lasted three days; Dworzecki, *Yerushalayim DeLita*, pp. 108–109, 121.

161 See Rudashevski, *Yomano Shel Na'ar MiVilna*, p. 28.

162 In the two *Gelbschein-Aktionen* of October 24, 1941, and of November 3–5, 1941, about 6,200 Jews altogether were caught and massacred; Kruk, *The Last Days*, p. 285; Einat, *Hayei Yom-Yom*, pp. 104–105. After three days of staying in the vacated Ghetto II, the holders of the yellow permits of Ghetto I were ordered to return. Several hundred Jews, who had hidden in *malinas* in Ghetto II since its liquidation, returned with them; Dworzecki, *Yerushalayim DeLita*, pp. 121–122.

had been inscribed as parents were detained, and the rest were released.[163] Indeed, hadn't they previously permitted this? And now it's a crime! This was apparently a practical joke for them: gathering up a few more people without much effort for Ponary.

The reregistration was very aggravating for me. I felt threatened that my name would be crossed off. I exerted all my strength to keep this from happening. That would have been a terrible blow for me. Felman also had to endure a lot on my account. They pounced on him, questioning him as to exactly why he had chosen to register me. They tried to force him to write in another woman who had some political connections and had requested during the registration that his permit be deferred. If you had connections among the [ghetto] authorities, anything was possible in the ghetto. I found out about this [the woman's connections], so I figured out exactly when they would be away, and I quickly slipped in and registered myself. Of course, most of all, what helped was Felman's goodwill. Without him, I would surely have been lost. My actions caused an uproar, but there was no way for them [the other woman and her connections] to cancel my registration as Felman's wife. I remained registered until the very end.[164] And in this manner, I was, as far as the ghetto authorities were concerned, a legal ghetto resident.

In the later *Aktionen,* the Germans didn't even bother to exert themselves. They relied on the Jews. The Germans would issue a demand that a certain number of Jews be provided, and the Jewish police themselves would gather up the required number. They could be depended upon. They would blow up the *malinas* and drag people out of all their little corners. They earned the trust of the Germans to such an extent that they were even sent into the provincial towns to round up people.[165]

---

163 According to Kruk, this occurred on December 15, 1941; Kruk, *The Last Days*, p. 286. Dworzecki, however, cites a different date—December 4; Dworzecki, *Yerushalayim DeLita*, pp. 83–84.

164 According to Dworzecki, the various permits were changed many times; Dworzecki, *Yerushalayim DeLita*, pp. 78–79.

165 This occurred much later, in May 1943, during the Kovno–Ponary *Aktion*, which the diarist mentioned in her entry on May 15, 1944.

Since I had a pink permit[166]—all those who were registered on a yellow permit also had pink permits—I was certain that the Jewish police would not bother me. As far as the Germans were concerned, none of us, not even the best artisan, was ever sure of his life. It was said that if you worked you were more secure. But I didn't count on this. There had been instances when, even at the work site itself, they would find some kind of minute fault, detain the person, and then that individual was never again seen in the ghetto.

Everyone wanted to earn something extra to live on. So people would carry out [of the ghetto] various things, their own or someone else's, to sell to the Christians. People would buy produce from the Christians. If you were caught in this kind of trade, you would be taken to Lukishki. Groups would be stopped on the road and searched often. One time they detained an entire group, mostly women, from the horticulture school. Every woman had hidden on her person several kilograms of flour. So they were taken away to prison. Only in rare instances did anyone manage to save himself. The singer Lyuba Zublevitzki was detained by Murer himself at the gate for having 2 kilograms of peas.[167] She worked in the *Schneiderstube*.[168] He conducted a complete investigation there and "proved" that she had stolen the peas. They took her away to Lukishki.

---

166 On the night of December 21, 1941, the ghetto police issued pink permits to all relatives of holders of a yellow permit, who previously had been issued blue passes that allowed them to remain in the ghetto. These permits, which were only valid inside the ghetto, were also issued to a few other people who were essential workers in the ghetto. Altogether about 3,000 permits were issued. See Balberyshski, *Shtarker fun ayzn*, pp. 150, 294–296; Dworzecki, *Yerushalayim DeLita*, pp. 78, 126.

167 As the right-hand man of the Vilna area commissar and the person in charge of Jewish affairs and supplies to the ghetto, Murer became a central and terrifying figure in the ghetto. He served there until he was sent to the front on June 30, 1943; Kruk, *The Last Days*, p. 580. Lyuba Zublevitzki, known more as Lyuba (Leah) Levitzka, was the beloved singer of the ghetto who was called the nightingale of the ghetto. She studied music at the Vienna Conservatory and was active in Jewish musical life in Vilna. In 1939–1941, she headed the solo singing class at the State Conservatory in Vilna. She appeared at ghetto concerts and conducted a class at the ghetto music school. She was murdered at Ponary in January 1943; Sutzkever, *Vilner ghett*o pp. 118–120; Balberyshski, *Shtarker fun ayzn*, p. 313; Dworzecki, *Yerushalayim DeLita*, pp. 165, 234; Rudashevski, *Yomano Shel Na'ar MiVilna*, pp. 91, 96.

168 This refers to the tailor workshop, where about 150 Jews worked.

None of the efforts by Gens or Dessler helped.[169] The story was told, and it is to be believed that they sent the bloodied clothes that she had been wearing to the *Schneiderstube.* Many similar incidents occurred. All these facts show that even if you worked, it didn't guarantee your life. I actually avoided working as long as possible. I didn't want to wear myself out for nothing. Felman brought in produce and I took care of the housekeeping. I actually became a housewife in the ghetto. I had never led such a peaceful kind of life, without a lot of running around...

Staying exclusively in the ghetto, however, was harder than going to work. By going out, you could at least briefly leave behind the ghetto atmosphere. We were always tense, never calm, always expecting something to happen. All of a sudden you would hear the ghetto police yell: "Go in through the gates." Then we would already know that one of our caregivers had arrived.[170] In the space of a minute, the streets would be emptied. All the windows and balcony doors would be closed. You risked being locked up in Lida Prison[171] if you glanced out the window. Such visits happened quite often. Especially, toward the end [of the ghetto's existence], when not a day would pass [without a visit], often several in the same day. The reaction to these visits was always the same fear. We could not get used to them. You never knew how such a visit might end. They might even go into the houses and seize everyone. There were many occasions when we ran away to hide. When Murer would drive up to the gate to catch people returning from work, everything would be confiscated already then [at the gate]. He would also bestow

---

169 Yakov Gens (1903–1943), former officer in the Lithuanian army, was a Zionist Revisionist, who was married to a non-Jewish Lithuanian woman. He worked as an accountant in the Lithuanian cooperative Lietukis and in the Vilna Municipal Health Department in the Soviet era. When the war broke out, he was serving as the acting superintendent of the Jewish hospital. During the first period of the ghetto's existence, he was the police commander. He later became the representative of the Vilna ghetto and the chief of police; Balberyshski, *Shtarker fun ayzn*, pp. 254, 425; Kruk, *The Last Days*, p. 305. Salek Dessler, born in Vilna, served as the liaison between the ghetto police and the Gestapo during the first period of the ghetto and later as the ghetto police commander. He openly collaborated with the Gestapo and was hated by all the ghetto inhabitants; Kruk, *The Last Days*, p. 327; Balberyshski, *Shtarker fun ayzn*, pp. 420–421, 425.

170 The diarist refers sarcastically to one of the high-level Germans.

171 This was the prison on Lida Alley, inside the ghetto, run by the Jewish police.

the honor of a blow from time to time. He wasn't too lazy even to show up before daybreak, at 5 or 6 A.M., to see how people were leaving the ghetto. One day he ordered everyone who came back from work to spread out everything they had with them, except for produce. They could not even withhold a single coin, under threat of being shot on the spot.[172] People suffered great losses that time. Some of them were carrying other people's money and had to make good the loss. Another time he detained the entire group of women from the *Schneiderstube* at the ghetto gate. Each one had to go into the guardhouse and strip naked. He himself stood by and forced the Jewish police to search them.

One day he actually sauntered into the women's bath. He would quite often visit the workshops in the ghetto and amuse himself in various sadistic ways, telling people to crawl under the table, or something like that, while at the same time expressing satisfaction with the orderliness and productivity, and boasting about how the Vilna ghetto took first place among all the ghettos.

Weren't we lucky!

Various German commissions would arrive often. One time they came to examine the sanitary condition of the courtyards, another time to check the cleanliness of the houses and, from time to time, to see if Jews were storing food reserves. Sometimes, they would come for no specific reason at all, just to observe how we lived. One time they even descended on us in the middle of the night, entering several houses, to see how we slept.[173] In this way, they never stopped being concerned about our welfare. On the other hand, the ghetto authorities took care to be prepared for such visits, so we also had to put up with them. People suffered from so many caregivers.

In the ghetto, there were three committees, commissioners, representatives, sergeants, assistant sergeants, special police, and ordinary police; also a court, criminal police, and a prison on Lida Alley that we dreaded as much as Lukishki Prison. There was a labor authority

172 See Balberyshski, *Shtarker fun ayzn*, p. 429; Rudashevski, *Yomano Shel Na'ar MiVilna*, pp. 71, 78, 82–83; Korchak, *Lehavot Ba'efer*, pp. 82–83; Rolnikaite, *Ani Hayevet Lesaper*, p. 51.

173 See Kruk, *The Last Days*, p. 119.

that operated as an intermediary with the German labor authority. This also was a "frightful" institution. Every lowlife idiot had a voice there. They did you a big favor if they even talked to you. They let themselves be bribed. Otherwise, you often had problems with them.

The Judenrat occupied the entire building of the former Real-Gymnasium.[174] There was a different department for every matter:[175] housing department, sanitation department, outdoor sanitation police, electricity department, finance department. In short: departments upon departments. There were directors, deputy directors, secretaries, assistant secretaries, and just "plain government" people. Reaching any given director was quite a difficult task.

There was a special institution for social welfare. They would provide rent subsidies and once a month they would distribute a few kilograms of potatoes, 2 kilograms of bread, a whole or half pound of peas, a little salt, and money—up to 100 rubles. They also gave out coupons, entitling you to get free soup from the kitchen; from time to time, a little bit of wood and free medical assistance. Some people even got free cots to sleep on. You had to submit a request. If the investigation determined that you were really in need, you would get a certain amount of help. It was very useful to have connections among these bureaucrats. In that case, your request would be handled more quickly. If not, it would drag on, even in urgent cases, for a much longer time.

There was even a sort of winter assistance, a special committee that went from house to house collecting clothes. Everyone who had even the slightest means had to contribute something. If someone had the

---

174 The Real-Gymnasium was a Jewish gymnasium in which classes were taught in Yiddish, under the auspices of the Zentraler Bildungs Komitet (Central Education Committee), which promoted Yiddish secular education in Vilna. It was located in the courtyard of 6 Rudnitzki Street. In 1933, the gymnasium received government recognition, and from then on the matriculation exams enabled the graduates to enroll in the university. In September 1941, the Judenrat of Ghetto I settled in the Real Gymnasium's building; Yisrael Kloizner, *Vilna Yerushalayim DeLita*: *Dorot Aharonim 1881–1939* (Hebrew) (Tel Aviv: Ghetto Fighters' House and Hakibbutz Hame'uhad, 1983), pp. 613, 616–619; Guzenberg, *Vilne*, pp. 197–199; Dworzecki, *Yerushalayim DeLita*, p. 71.

175 Regarding the organization of the ghetto administration and the functions of the various departments, see Balberyshski, *Shtarker fun ayzn*, pp. 300–419.

resources but didn't want to donate, the police would take it from him by force. All the clothes would be gathered together at a designated location where they would be distributed. Here too connections were essential. Without it, you would have to wait in line for days and in the end all you got was a rag. If you had access to the authorities, things looked totally different. But in general, you had to admit that the order in the ghetto was exemplary. However, their attitude toward everyone was very unsympathetic—it was a harsh dictatorship.

Also included in the "winter assistance," were the clothes of all of those people who, instead of going to Kovno, were taken to a closer place—to Ponary.[176] This time the Germans quite openly gave away the clothes. They toyed with us. Before [the true destination was revealed], they had given people the opportunity to carry as much as they wanted in wagons. Not everyone was permitted to travel to Kovno, only the younger people, all the more to mask the trap. Afterwards, all these clothes were brought back to the ghetto in wagons. This made a frightful impression on everyone. Just two days earlier, these people had walked through the ghetto for hours on end "to the train." People stood by the windows and watched them. I was no longer looking then. I couldn't stand to watch it. I maintained that they were voluntarily going to their deaths. Yisrolik happened to be at my place. He also stepped away from the window and wept. He also had the same opinion as I did.

Why did Kovno need so many Jews? Most of these people really believed that they were going to Kovno. After all the signing up and all the formalities, it was logical to think so. Before, people wanted to delude themselves, that maybe those who were taken out somewhere were still alive? This time there was no way to fool yourself. It was clear and obvious.

Every *Aktion* had a different set of criteria. One time there was a demand to provide a certain number of old people. The older women dyed their gray hair black so as to appear younger. The younger ones moved

---

176 The diarist refers to the clothes of the murdered people of the Kovno–Ponary *Aktion*, which the Germans sent as "gifts" for the neediest in the ghetto. Of course, the Lithuanian murderers and the nearby peasants first took the best items for themselves. Not everyone in the ghetto felt it was proper to take the clothes of the dead. See Kruk, *The Last Days*, p. 505; Balberyshski, *Shtarker fun ayzn*, p. 457.

about freely and the older ones hid. Often it was just the opposite. That time, the Jewish police rounded up about 400 people. They actually took them to Pospieshk for a vacation, kept them there for about a week, and fed them well. After that they disappeared. In what manner—no one knew.[177] In the ghetto it was said that the police had taken mostly people who were sick, living alone, who had no means of support, and who were receiving subsidies. So a lot of people stopped turning to social welfare for help. That's how they would carry out small *chistkes* from time to time, and ghetto life would go on in its own unique way.

Besides these *chistkes*, there would often be other kinds of *Aktionen*. One time, they were going around checking to see if anyone had more than 300 rubles. Any excess rubles were confiscated by the Jewish police. No amount of pleading helped. Their response was that everything always had to be in order, which meant that if you had more than the allowed limit, you had to make sure that it wasn't found. Each person had the right to have only 300 rubles.[178] Any extra had to be given to the Germans. In the most normal times in the ghetto, a kilogram of bread cost 25 rubles, a kilogram of potatoes also cost 25 rubles. So was it really possible to survive on such an amount...

At one point, they went from house to house confiscating copper. Then there was the matter of furs. A proclamation was issued to surrender all furs. If even a scrap of fur was found with anyone, they threatened to shoot the whole courtyard. So people voluntarily turned in their furs to the Judenrat, whatever they had, even their plain fur jackets. The Jewish police went to every home to check for furs. Afterwards, the Lithuanians also came and carried out searches in every house.[179] So people were

---

177 On July 17, 1942, more than eighty elderly people were brought to the former building of the OZE—Obshchestvo Zdravo'okhraneniya Yevreyev (Society for the Safeguarding of Jews' Health)—children's camp in the Pospiesk Forest, which was named after Doctor Zemach Shabad, on 10 Gurantzy Street (today 55A Žirgo Street). For more on the camp, see Guzenberg, *Vilne*, pp. 660–661. The Jewish ghetto police brought them bread and other products daily. After nine days, they were taken to their death in Ponary; Einat, *Hayei Yom-Yom*, p. 313; Kruk, *The Last Days*, pp. 330, 338; Balberyshski, *Shtarker fun ayzn*, p. 451.

178 This order had been issued already before the establishment of the ghettos, presumably on September, 1, 1941; Sutzkever, *Vilner ghetto* p. 33.

179 See Kruk, *The Last Days*, pp. 143–148.

always afraid. You never knew what else they would latch onto to bother you with. Once they actually took away chairs. But this was an internal ghetto order. They always found something new.

Regardless of all of this, there was a children's school and a daycare center in the ghetto, where mothers who went to work could leave their children who were at least two years old until 5 P.M. In the children's home, children were left overnight to sleep.[180] There was medical supervision everywhere. There was a trade school for the young people and courses for adults.[181] People often listed a trade on their [work] permit that they knew absolutely nothing about. These courses gave a person the opportunity to become more or less familiar with a specific trade in a short time. The library and the Jewish hospital were in the ghetto. There was a pharmacy near the hospital. In addition, a laboratory was set up that included a dentist's office and X-ray equipment.[182] There were two baths with showers and disinfectant stations. Everyone's clothes underwent disinfection.[183]

Going to the bathhouse once a month was obligatory, whereupon you received a note, stamped with the date that you were there. Without this stamp, you could not get a bread ration card.[184] In several kitchens, they distributed soup twice a week. A portion cost 5 rubles. Some people got it for free. You could also get boiled water and coffee there. Toward the end, this was available all day long.[185]

A capital renovation was implemented in Yankelevitch's former store, and a kind of café was set up.[186] You could drink coffee from five in the

---

180 See Dworzecki, *Yerushalayim DeLita*, pp. 208; 227–228; 232–233; Kruk, *The Last Days*, pp. 351–352.

181 Dworzecki, *Yerushalayim DeLita*, pp. 234–235; Kruk, *The Last Days*, pp. 233–234, 240–241; 469.

182 See Balberyshski, *Shtarker fun ayzn*, pp. 363–369; Dworzecki, *Yerushalayim DeLita*, p. 205.

183 See Dworzecki, *Yerushalayim DeLita*, p. 197; Balberyshski, *Shtarker fun ayzn*, pp. 381–385.

184 Balberyshski, *Shtarker fun ayzn*, p. 382; Korchak, *Lehavot Ba'efer*, p. 78.

185 On soup kitchens in the ghetto, see Kruk, *The Last Days*, pp. 244–245, 376; Dworzecki, *Yerushalayim DeLita*, p. 177–178.

186 On the café houses in the ghetto, see Dworzecki, *Yerushalayim DeLita*, pp. 179–180.

morning until late in the evening there. They also served dinners there consisting of two dishes, a kasha or some sort of hodgepodge, and a soup. This cost around 20 rubles and you had to turn in your produce ration card. Police got a discount. The place was fixed up luxuriously: two rooms, one quite large, with lots of small chairs and tables, all matching. A chandelier with many lights was turned on in the evening. At times, someone would play the piano, but this seemed somewhat out of place with the coffee and sugar in clay cups. The café was used as a meeting place. Had it not been for the yellow patches on the front and back [of the clothing of those there] and all the weary faces, a person could forget that he was in a ghetto. There was even a theater in the ghetto. From time to time, there were also concerts.[187] There were quite a number of attendees and the place was always packed. It seemed strange to me back then how people could have the fortitude to see a play or hear a concert when living in a cemetery.[188] But now I think that perhaps they were right. Fixating on everything that was going on around us would have made it impossible to go on living. So you had to distract yourself and push it out of your head as much as possible. Today, all those theatergoers are no longer here. So at least they took advantage of whatever was available.

In the streets or by the courtyard gates when the police chased them away, women would sell rye cookies, white rolls, cigarettes, and candies.[189] There were several confectionaries. There was a sort of open-air market in a courtyard on Shpitol Street. There they would sell various trifles: shoe polish made in the ghetto, matches, pins, and much more. There were several bakeries. For a certain fee, a pot of food could be cooked up for you. You brought it in early in the morning before going to work and picked it up at 4 or 5 P.M. Many private homes also baked bread to sell.

---

187 On theaters and concerts, see Dworzecki, *Yerushalayim DeLita*, pp. 244–245, 248–254; Kruk, *The Last Days*, pp. 250, 271, 342, 368, 377–378, 553–554.

188 Flyers were distributed in the ghetto with the text: You do not create theater in a graveyard; Dworzecki, *Yerushalayim DeLita*, p. 249. According to Kruk, the Bundists did this; Kruk, *The Last Days*, p. 174. According to Kremerman, religious Jews did this; Kremerman, *MiVilna,* "*Yerushalayim DeLita*," p. 102.

189 See Kruk, *The Last Days*, pp. 158, 242–243, 275; Dworzecki, *Yerushalayim DeLita*, pp. 168–169.

There were several shops and special places that sold meat, sometimes also fish. All of these places were located in the courtyards.

Everyone had a hiding place. In the event that outsiders came into the ghetto, they cleared everything out, without leaving a trace.

You could get everything in the shops: butter, eggs, cheese, sour cream, small herrings, sausages, various vegetables, tomatoes, apples, berries, fresh rolls, even sweet rolls. There were also people who went house-to-house offering various goods. Their prices were lower than those in the stores. Only a select few could afford items such as butter, meat, fish, and similar products. So it was often hard to dispose of such products. For the most part, the ghetto survived by smuggling things in and hiding them in the *malinas*. There they would stash bags of potatoes, flour, sides of meat, and baskets of fish.

Sometimes the *malinas* were discovered and walled up. In that case, new ones would be dug out. As long as they were allowed to live, Jews figured out a way to cope with their situation. At times, they would make arrangements with the police: they bribed the Lithuanian who stood guard at the gate and would bring in produce through the gate, hidden under some wood. Over time, the risks associated with these endeavors became ever greater.

Toward the end, we were only numbers to the Germans. All the permits were replaced with a sort of tin tag with an engraved number. This was the main document. Everyone had to wear this tag on a string around his neck.[190] When someone was detained, it often happened that he would be released and then detained once more by someone checking the number tags. In the last months, they would arrest not only the "criminal," but also his entire family. They arrested a chimney sweep and the police also had to hand over his two young children. In this way, in addition to the *chistkes*, they carried out constant annihilation. There were always new victims. There were people who would have died of hunger had they not taken risks. So they didn't restrain themselves. Their choice

---

190 The Jews called it the "hound number." Those with a tag also had to have a yellow permit in the ghetto; see Dworzecki, *Yerushalayim DeLita*, p. 80. For a photo of such a tag, see ibid., p. 447. See also Rudashevski, *Yomano Shel Na'ar MiVilna*, p. 93.

was to die either this way, or to die that way. Whenever they clamped down at the ghetto gate, everything in the ghetto became scarce. Then you couldn't get a kilogram of bread or a potato to save your life. Those who were better off were able to prepare for such days by stockpiling food. But those who barely got through each day suffered terribly during such times. The economic conditions of individuals varied widely. The smugglers earned well. You couldn't make a living from bringing in a few pounds of potatoes and some pieces of bread, but if you sold off half, the other half could be considered your profit. And how often it was that they confiscated everything at the gate![191] How often it happened that those at home would sit all day without eating, waiting for a few potatoes, and then people would come home empty-handed. This occurred frequently. In such cases, the tragedy was much greater than for those whose confiscated items were butter, meat, or other luxury items. They would be able to cope with such a setback more easily. But in the other cases, it was simply a great misfortune. There were even cases where food had been bought with borrowed money that then had to be paid back.

There were some people who still had valuable objects and money, so they could indulge in a good life. Others, a select few, had worked their way up thanks to the liquidated ghetto.[192] The Germans had turned over to these Jews the task of carrying the contents from the abandoned dwellings into the warehouses. They took advantage of that opportunity to help themselves. Some of them, mainly police, subsisted on these things during that whole period. I went there once [to the other ghetto].[193] It made a terrible impression on me. The houses were open and things were scattered all over the place. In one house, I found plates with food on the table, as if they had just a moment before gone out for a short while. I took a teakettle and several plates with me and immediately ran out.

However, there were also people who had absolutely nothing at all to live on. Even the small rations of butter and sugar that were handed out once, sometimes twice, a month were never kept for one's own use, but

---

191 See Balberyshski, *Shtarker fun ayzn*, pp. 429–430; Kruk, *The Last Days*, p. 284.

192 This refers to Ghetto II, the Small Ghetto.

193 On that occasion, the diarist visited Mrs. Arlyuk's tenant in order to get back from her some of the things that she had entrusted to her.

instead were sold, and the money was used to buy a few kilograms of bread. The aid from social welfare could at best suffice for one person for only two days. Be that as it may, a family consists of several people and a month has not two but thirty days. So, indeed, many people gave up standing in the lines and did not even bother turning to welfare for any help at all.

There were also those who would go begging for alms. Such people, however, were very few in number. The community did not accept this at all. On the contrary, people wanted to save face, to maintain their privacy, and to suffer in silence. People would go hungry and freeze, sitting all winter long in an unheated room, covering themselves with whatever they had available. It was not uncommon for children to ask for something to eat, and there was not even a crumb of bread to be found in the house. I remember how one time, on the steps of my friend's house, a three-year-old girl was crying and screaming: "I want to eat!" Her mother hit her and told her to go to sleep. So then I brought her something to eat. She grabbed the food and devoured it so quickly that as they say, even stones would have wept upon observing such a scene. When did it ever happen that such a dear little soul, even in the worst of times [before the war], knew such hunger?

It was impossible to survive from just the bread ration cards, even if you had a supplemental card because you worked. The employees of the Judenrat had additional rations, but that was also not enough. They were not able to leave the ghetto and so were forced to pay twice the price. There were also "iron" rations—whole, halves, and quarters. People who were granted such rations received a certain amount of bread, sugar, butter, and various other products every week. Only very few people received whole rations. Senior officials received halves and quarters.[194]

---

194 According to Balberyshski, there were weekly rations no. 1, 2, 3, 4 and 5, which varied in sizes and distribution. Ration no. 1 was the biggest and it was only given to the five leading members of the Judenrat. The size of rations decreased and the number of recipients increased with no. 2, 3, 4 and 5. There were also split rations, amounting to three quarters, halves, and quarters of ration no. 5. For more on these rations, see Balberyshski, *Shtarker fun ayzn*, pp. 330–331. In regard to the diarist's use of the word "iron," she probably referred to the German term "eiserne Ration" (iron ration, which usually refers to a small supply of food that is stored and used only as a last resort), though not using it in the original meaning.

This was already a huge subsidy. But those who received these extra rations already had the means to survive even without this additional support. These supplementary rations were created by taking a small portion from each person's bread ration card. Bread ration cards were distributed by house administrators and the block commanders.

Every courtyard had a house administrator, a block commander, and a guard. In addition, every dwelling had its own female or male commander.[195] There was no shortage of titles in the ghetto. They even wanted to recruit me as a block commander, but I wriggled out of it. I didn't want to be bothered with a title in the ghetto, and on top of that, to have bureaucrats ordering me around. Later on I had a few regrets, since this would have given me some privileges. I did have the honor of being a dwelling commander, quite a low position. Every once in a while, this resulted in some unpleasant moments for me: for example, I would have an argument with a neighbor concerning who was on duty that day to clean the kitchen or the stairs. There were other such similar petty things. One time I even had to spend a whole night in Lida Prison. The person who cleaned the kitchen had left some dust on the electric meter, so she and I, being responsible, were both punished.

Every day the block commander, a woman, would come to see that the dwellings were in order. A woman who was responsible for sanitation would come several times a week. From time to time, a whole commission of sanitation police with a sanitation doctor at the helm would show up. In the crowded conditions in which we found ourselves, it was imperative to oversee hygiene. But it was difficult to always maintain ideal order. There were six of us living together in a tiny room that measured exactly 12 meters. During the day, only two beds were left open. At night, we would open the other beds. To pass through, you had to crawl over the others. It was actually a bit of an advantage that ours was the last room.[196] In the other passageway-rooms, it was really awful, like a fair. In our room itself, I had a little stovetop, made from an oven, with pipes along the length of the room, and this is what I used to cook.

---

195 Ibid., p. 379.

196 The apartment was apparently a railroad apartment, also known as a shotgun apartment.

I kept wood, potatoes, and whatever else I had in this room, and I was glad to have them. The others also kept everything in the room. Our leaders demanded that the rooms always be kept neat and always be ready to receive the German commissions. But that would have meant not cooking, not eating, and, in general, not living. We were permitted to cook only what we had received with our ration cards. No other products were allowed in the house. When the Germans came, they would sometimes stir the pot with a spoon to see what was cooking. So we would hide everything whenever they showed up. But our own committee would come totally unexpectedly, and there wouldn't be any warning shouts: "Go inside the gates." That's when our people caused us real aggravation.

Our chief inspector of dwellings once poured out a whole pot of cooked food because it was too good! At another place, he confiscated a *kvashine*.[197] He used to say that you could cook and eat anything, as long as it wasn't discovered. If they found a pot that had not been thoroughly scoured, even if it had just been taken off the stove [after being used to cook some food], they would confiscate it. Any protests would be useless. All their decisions were beyond any appeal. They would say that you should treat them just as if it was the Germans who had come. This is how they wanted to take care of the ghetto. This gave the impression that some of them had become so caught up in their power that they had forgotten that they too were Jews and that they also found themselves in the ghetto. It seems to me that even under the best of conditions this was hard to forget. You only had to go out in the streets and see the high fence.

I am sure that this same Mr. Oster,[198] upon coming home from his inspections, did not have to eat black *burtchak*[199] for dinner, nor did he have to eat rotten cabbage, nor frozen potatoes, dripping with water, nor stinking horse meat, which was considered to be a holiday treat when you

---

197 This may be a Russian word for a type of bucket used to ferment dough.

198 Here and in the previous paragraph, this is a reference to Raphael Oster, a Kovno Jew, who was the head of the sanitation police and the Housing Department in the ghetto. Later he became the leader of the criminal police; Dworzecki, *Yerushalayim DeLita*, p. 149.

199 *Burtchak*, originally from the Turkish, was used in parts of the Soviet Union as a term for beans, peas, or foraged alternatives.

actually managed to get some. And certainly, he didn't have to hide his food and could eat openly at a table.

Instead of a friendly attitude on the part of our own people, we were subjected to repulsive brutality from them. On one occasion, they punished our entire courtyard for damaging the restroom. The reason it broke down was a technical one. But that didn't make any difference. We yelled, we protested, but it was like talking to the wall. Every family had to pay 100 rubles. There were about 200 families. Quite a tidy sum. A few people, with tears [in their eyes], barely managed to get an agreement to pay only 50 percent. Whoever didn't pay was taken to Lida Prison. I refused to pay, preferring to sit in jail. That's how we experienced more aggravation.

In the ghetto, renovations were always going on. They "took good care" of us.[200] The Germans, concerned for our welfare, wanted to make us more comfortable with more living space. So they assigned Yatkever Street and a few more courtyards, including Yanovski's, to us.[201] The apartments would be remodeled and people would move in. The workshops operated in three shifts, day and night, without stopping. They took over more and more locations. There was talk that all of the front-facing apartments on Rudnitzki Street would be emptied of its tenants and would be taken over for workshops. Most of the production was in support of the German army. A few months before the liquidation, the Germans were still bringing in new sewing machines to the tailor shops. People comforted themselves with the notion that this was proof that the ghetto would continue to exist. The Germans didn't lose anything by this action. The machines remained in place.

People would start gathering to go to work at around five in the morning. Rudnitzki Street would start humming. Every [work] unit assembled at a different courtyard gate. The head was called the brigadier. There were also column leaders, who were authorized to direct the various groups.

---

200 This refers to the restoration of ruins, warehouses, cellars, and attics that was taken care of by the Housing Department in the ghetto—not by the Germans—in order to create more apartments; ibid., p. 148.

201 Besides the new courtyards on Yatkever Street, Dworzecki also mentioned courtyards on Disna Street, Oshmener Street, and German Street; ibid., p. 148.

The groups were not allowed to go [out of the ghetto] alone [without their leader]. A few larger units that worked at multiple sites had several column leaders. In the final months, they even instituted foremen, people who were responsible for groups of ten workers and who made sure that no one was missing.

Before leaving the ghetto, the brigadier would drop the list of people whom he was taking out and a separate list of those who were absent into a little box by the gate. The labor police took those [who were absent] who did not have an excuse from a doctor to Lida Prison. Employees of the labor administration would stand at the gate and count how many people went out, checking to see that their count agreed with the list. And they would count again upon the workers' return. This was not done at the beginning. Only later, when they began to notice that some people were escaping into the forests to join the partisans, did they institute this procedure. There had been several instances when Lithuanians or Germans had caught the fugitives along the way. After that, they issued orders to maintain strict surveillance to ensure that no one should escape from the ghetto.

I could never get used to the sight of people lining up three or four in a row, with their yellow patches, some made from the coarse sackcloth used for overalls, others simply torn off rags. Women who worked in the gardens had to travel many kilometers to get to work.[202] They would leave around 5 A.M. and return late in the evening, sometimes even as late as 10 P.M. with bloodied and swollen feet, carrying the few bits of vegetables that they had managed to buy, and trembling with anxiety lest they be confiscated at the gate.

The brigadier would collect the wages, a trivial amount, and pay everybody. A certain percentage of the wages had to be paid to the Judenrat. They issued tax booklets in which the taxes that were paid were recorded. If you didn't pay the tax, they would detain your ration cards.

One time, already near the end, everyone was forced to work a certain amount of time at the railway station. Even Judenrat employees were required to work there one day a month. My neighbors often had to work there, on some occasions as many as ten days a month. I was the only

202 It is not clear what the diarist means by gardens; perhaps public gardens or parks.

one who didn't get such a notice. Apparently, totally by chance, they had overlooked me. I certainly did not suffer any regrets from this oversight. The work there was hard, especially in the freezing winter. The Germans stood over you while you worked on the rails, pressing you to work harder, and often delivering blows.

One morning, when people were already starting to assemble to go to work, there was suddenly a panic. No one knew what was going on. People looked at each other and then ran away to hide. It turned out that Estonians had encircled the ghetto. Soon they burst into the ghetto. They attacked us like a pack of hungry wolves and captured the men. They labored at this all day. The Jewish police were also mobilized to help out.

In the evening, I went to the ghetto gate to look through the crack to see if anybody was there. All of a sudden, the gate opened and I saw a German. I remained hidden behind a small door. If I stayed where I was, he would nab me. So, I slowly began to edge myself out of there. He spotted me, pointed his rifle at me, and set off after me, just like a dogcatcher chasing a dog. Of course, he could have dealt with me harshly, but at that time they were only interested in catching men. So he just gave me a warning. You can imagine the terror that I experienced in those few moments. Barely breathing, I ran up the stairs [to my apartment].

In addition to the *chapunes*, the labor authority was continuously seizing people for [deportation to] Estonia. The first to be selected were those who had come from the provinces. Notices were sent to them, and there was nothing they could do about it.[203] The longer this continued [the nabbing of people for Estonia], the more it began to assume a mass character. They would send out whole families, even those with small children. Only in a few instances did some people manage to buy their way out by paying huge sums of money to remain in the ghetto. All those who were released from a large group of work units were sent to work at the railway station. Felman too was among them. Some days he would go to work, other days he stayed home. It just so happened that on that day [when Felman did not go to work], Gens made a speech in which he

---

203 This presumably refers to the second transport to Estonia on August 24, 1943, when 1,400 Jews were transported, including the Jews from the province who had arrived in the ghetto in March 1943; see Einat, *Hayei Yom Yom*, p. 320.

demanded that people check that no one was absent. If someone didn't return at night [with their work group], it was to be reported right away. Otherwise, the whole house would have to answer for it.

At night, an uproar started when news spread that the police were conducting raids in search of those who had not been to work that day. It smelled of Estonia. Felman hid. I also wanted to hide. After all, I was his official wife, so I was certainly also responsible. But the neighbors stubbornly refused to let me go: "Gens ordered that no one should be let out."

Make your report and let me out [I replied]. Not only did they not let me out, but they even reported that Felman was missing. Even now it makes me laugh when I recall how the whole house, about twenty people, followed me around step by step. I got angry and went to my room, got undressed, and lay down in bed. They all remained in the courtyard, watching to make sure that I didn't leave. Of course, I wasn't able to sleep. As soon as they made their report, I was sure that the authorities would soon arrive. Sure enough, a few hours later, two policemen came looking for Felman. Not finding him, they took me!

The police station was packed. The despair was great. People were shoving each other, weeping and distraught. I, being a calm prisoner, was placed on the unblocked side [outside of the cell]. The commissioner, Bernstein,[204] came over to me and, in a suspicious tone, asked if I knew where Felman was. He knew Felman and knew that I wasn't his real wife. I actually knew where Felman was, but I wasn't about to give him away. Bernstein didn't leave me alone. Again he came over and warned me that I was in danger of sacrificing myself on account of Felman. I simply answered him that there was nothing I could do to help. I didn't want to demean myself by asking him to let me go. I knew that would be pointless. These people would often respond that they were not people, just police. I took advantage of an opportunity and sent a message to

204 Leo Bernstein was a Zionist communal worker. He first was a policeman, later a teacher, and finally the director of the Cultural Department in the ghetto. He was primarily active in Hebrew cultural work and was the director of the youth club. When Gens fired him after two months, on June 26, 1943, he apparently returned to his police post; Dworzecki, *Yerushalayim DeLita*, p. 224; Kruk, *The Last Days*, pp. 525, 535, 577.

Yosef, Felman's brother, to try to get me released. After all, he had also once been some kind of a policeman. But he didn't make any effort.

So I sat and pondered this, and this is what ran through my thoughts: I'd saved myself from death so many times! The very first day that the Germans came into the postal courtyard, the time of the provocation,[205] the time when I was detained by a German for not wearing the patches, which meant certain death, he freed me from a Lithuanian police station. I eluded several *chistkes* when I was still in the other ghetto, and I even survived the final liquidation [of Ghetto II]. And now, to fall into the hands of our own Jews! Oh well, what's the use. This, apparently, is the end for me; that was what I was thinking.

The neighbors were sorry; they felt guilty. So they looked for Felman. It would be some military justice to free me and to hand him over!

The police kept on bringing in new people. One of them, a woman, the sister of Rabinovitch, who had owned the shoe store on Vilna Street, was brought in wearing her nightgown. Apparently, she had not wanted to go, so they dragged her in by force. Such diligent workers!

Daylight was beginning to break when they opened the door and told everyone to go. I didn't hurry. Why should I push myself? I won't be late for Lida. So one of the policemen called out, "Why are you sitting here? You can leave." I left. It turned out that they had released everyone, both from the police station and from Lida.

As I understand it, the police were playing a little game. They were having a difficult time gathering and delivering the required number of people [to send to Estonia], so they decided, in the meantime, to release all the detainees. The threatened [Jews] made a dash for work and soon, before even reaching the train on Ponaryski Street, people were seized, both men and women, and packed into caged wagons that had been prepared in advance. Felman was also among those sent that day.

I talked to him and advised him not to go. When he went out on the street and saw that everyone was going—there were several thousand people—he also joined the line and departed. I had a feeling that things would not go smoothly. There were apparently some in the ghetto who knew what was going on. As soon as the work groups had gone out of the

205 The diarist refers to "The First Great Provocation" on August 31, 1941.

ghetto, pandemonium broke out. Many ran away. Those who came back into the ghetto were detained by the police and turned in. Felman also ran away and came back into the ghetto, but not until the fourth day. But what good did it do him? Exactly two months later, the Jewish police dragged him out of his *malina*.[206] They didn't even let him stay for a minute in the courtyard so I could give him a package. They immediately led him to a truck that was waiting outside the ghetto by the gate. I went over to a German and asked him to let me approach Felman. They weren't bothering women at that particular time. So the German allowed me to go. Isn't that a laugh? This German turned out to be more sympathetic than the Jews.

The police were "toiling" away then. They went in groups with large pocket lamps and axes in their hands, and banged on the walls, hacking away and tearing them down. They destroyed several walls. There were also several victims. Very likely, this was done by order of the Germans.

The Germans themselves must be laughing at us. Not only did they not have to bother themselves with us, nor did they have to pay the Lithuanians per head the way they had done before there was a ghetto,[207] but among the Jews themselves they had loyal collaborators. The Jews would fill their quota, however many the Germans wanted. Wouldn't it have been better to refuse to do this work and let the Germans do it themselves? It's possible that the liquidation might then have come about sooner. It's also possible that some of those who were able to save themselves, including myself, would have fallen in [the German–Lithuanian net of *Aktionen*]. Well, so what, in addition to the many thousands [who perished], there would have been a few hundred more! How are we better than the others? But then at least [if the Jewish police had refused to fill the quota] we would not have been spitting on ourselves.

How were the Jewish police any different from the Lithuanian *chapunes*? Did they at least in some way ease the situation? What did they accomplish by being the ones to do the capturing? The way I see it, they were only looking out for themselves until the very end. What then can we demand of other nations? In a time of such pain, of such humiliation,

---

206 The time period that is specified seems to be wrong, since the Estonia *Aktionen* began in August 1943, and the ghetto was liquidated on September 23, 1943.

207 They paid the Lithuanians 10 rubles per head before there was a ghetto.

all you saw from them was arrogance and impudence. Even those same evil decrees could have been carried out in a more courteous manner, at least a little more gently. Some despicable pipsqueak policeman from a small Lithuanian shtetl, wearing leather gloves, his nose in the air, would give you a push, saying, "Faster, go faster!" He might also beat you sometimes.

I personally never had anything to do with them. But looking at one of them, I wanted to spit in his face and smack his fat cheeks.

In the worst period of antisemitism in Poland, people could commit the worst acts, and still the official comportment was courteous, even with the political arrestees. If a real Jewish state is ever established, according to the same pattern of the ghetto "government," then it will be better that it never exists. It's easier to suffer at the hands of strangers.

What was Gens thinking when he made those reassuring speeches that the ghetto stood on secure ground and that there was no threat of danger while at the same time turning in thousands of heads? I never heard him [speak]. I couldn't stomach it. For me, it was enough just to hear what people said about the speeches. Did he actually believe his own speeches? Maybe he hoped that by giving up a portion he would gain time and save the rest? I understand quite well that his role was a difficult one. I don't feel I have the right to accuse him. For that, you would have to know precisely all the details, the situations, and the demands of the Germans. I don't know how things were conducted in other ghettos. Maybe it had to be this way. But I cannot in any way agree with it. When one of the top leaders resisted and refused to go to the provinces and conduct operations to round up people, Gens punished him by sending him out of the ghetto [to a labor camp] to do peat work.[208]

---

208 This refers to Yosef Glazman (1908–1943), head of the Lithuanian Beitar from 1938 and one of the most active leaders of the FPO, the underground partisan organization in the ghetto. All the ghetto inhabitants liked him. For a certain time, he was the deputy commander of the ghetto police. After he was fired, Gens nominated him as the head of the Housing Department in the ghetto. The diarist refers here to his arrest on November 1, 1942, for not carrying out Gens' order. He was supposed to be sent to a forest labor camp in Sorok-Tatar. Glazman was arrested once again on June 26, 1943, to be sent to do peat work in Reshe, but he was released by FPO members. On July 24, 1943, he led a group of partisans out of the ghetto; he was killed in the forest in a battle with the Germans on October 9, 1943; Kruk, *The Last Days*, pp. 398–399, 400, 402, 573–575; Balberyshski, *Shtarker fun ayzn*, pp. 421, 432.

It cannot be said that by carrying out the German demands, Gens was trying to save his own life. If that was his purpose, he certainly had better options than to remain in the ghetto, especially since his wife was Lithuanian. It is said that when they called him to the Gestapo, there were Lithuanians who were prepared to help him escape.[209] But he declined the offer with the excuse that this went against his honor as an officer. He had once been an officer in the Lithuanian army. So that means that it wasn't his own life that he was concerned about. In the name of honor, he allowed himself to be shot.[210] So why did he force us to defile our own overall honor [as a people]?

It's probably ludicrous to speak of honor after all that was perpetrated and after finding myself in such a dishonorable situation. Nevertheless, I still feel within myself a kind of defiant pride. It reminds me of the woman in a ballad by Mickiewicz, who never let herself be persuaded of anything, always sticking to her own opinion.[211] She got into an argument with her husband: he said that the dog had been shaved, she said that the dog had been shorn. Drowning in the river, already up to her neck in water, she still stretched out her hand and, lifting [two of] her fingers, showed him that it had been shorn. That is how it is with me...

I am homeless, alone, broken, living under a leaky roof that lets the rain pour down on my head in even the lightest shower. My only company, mice who surround me on all sides, very close neighbors, constantly squealing, and whom I am deathly afraid of from way back. Still, I stick to my opinion. So it's even more painful for me. I feel a deep hatred for

---

209 For other examples of rumors in circulation, see Balberyshski, *Shtarker fun ayzn*, pp. 474–475.

210 According to Balberyshski, this occurred on September 13, 1943; Balberyshski, *Shtarker fun ayzn*, pp. 474–475. According to Korchak, this occurred on September 14, 1943; Korchak, *Lehavot Ba'efer*, p. 193. Kittel convened the Jewish police and explained that Gens had been shot because he had not complied with the German authorities' orders; Balberyshski, *Shtarker fun ayzn*, p. 475.

211 This is a reference to the poem "Golono, Strzyżono" (Shaved, Sheared) by the Polish poet Adam Mickiewicz (1798–1855), which was based on a satirical tale with the same name by the Polish Baroque poet and writer Wacław Potocki (1622–1696). The poem describes how an insignificant marital quarrel led to the drowning of the wife in a pond at the hands of the husband.

those Jewish *chapunes*. If I should manage to survive, I don't ever want to meet any of them.

The fact that we were humiliated [by the Germans], that is an entirely different issue. But we ourselves should not have behaved like that, and in my opinion, that leaves a stain of shame on the history of our ghetto.[212]

[June 22, 1944]

Today is June 22, 1944, the third anniversary since the Germans entered Vilna,[213] and we are still not rid of them. From the first day that they arrived, it always seemed to me that any minute now they would be driven out. I have been waiting like this the whole time. Lately, the Christian woman has again begun talking about politics. People are saying that the end of the war is very near. Who knows how to understand this, very near? I would be happy if it ended, at least, by the end of autumn, just so long as it doesn't drag on for another winter. You might think that that's not such a long time, just four months. But for me, under these current conditions, another four months in this barn would be like four normal years. That it should be less than four months, I dare not even think about, for fear that my disappointment will be even greater. So be it [only four months].

Today it is actually 270 days that I find myself here in the village;[214] 270 days that I've been sleeping without a pillow or a blanket, ready at any minute to run away. It would be a real miracle if the Germans were to get out of here and in the process "*na zvamanie karku*."[215] So go make it happen! One thing, at least, did turn out as I had prayed for: that on this anniversary they should be regaled with a bunch of bombs. And that's how it was. Airplanes circled all day long. I heard about twenty loud explosions. I'm sure that they dropped more than that. After all, they

---

212 The first notebook of the diary ends here.

213 The Germans entered Vilna on June 24, 1941. The diarist actually referred to the German invasion of Lithuania on June 22, 1941.

214 The diarist entered the barn on September 27, 1943, that is, 270 days before the date of this entry, June 22, 1944.

215 An idiomatic Polish phrase, *na złamanie karku*, may be translated as: break their necks.

aren't just flying around on some outing. But probably the noise from the more distant explosions did not reach to here. So for now, I content myself with that thought.

On June 17 and 19, the bombing went on for several hours without stopping. One day I counted fifty-six explosions. I thought the Soviets were already here. And now more than two months have passed and still nothing.[216] From that time on, I don't attribute too much significance to the airplanes that circle all day long, often even at night, nor to the bombs that they drop from time to time. There's still no end in sight. This could play out for another half a year or even longer. Nevertheless, on days when I don't hear the hum of their planes, I feel somewhat sadder. No matter what, they still give me a reason to hope. After all, they didn't even come at all in the first two and a half years. That means that they are now also thinking about our region. Maybe, in the end, something will finally come out of this.

Today I read a newspaper dated June 21 [1944]. Just as vacuous as the one I read three weeks ago. Again, about the criminal conduct of the Soviets in dealing with the Polish population. One sees right away that these are lies. Most of the newspaper, starting from the first page, is full of brag about the newly developed bomb that they have launched to bomb London, how England is terrified of it, how they can no longer sleep calmly at night, and how the English themselves recognize the gruesomeness of the bomb. But they comfort themselves that this is Germany's last attempt before going under. Of course, they write this with irony. But in this situation, I prefer to believe in England. They write that the time has now come to settle accounts with England, as they promised the German people. Thanks to the new bomb, the air warfare will now take a whole new direction. This is exactly what occurred earlier when the first tanks appeared. There are many long articles dedicated to this subject, and they are all written in the form of short stories. One can't help laughing at this. Apparently, they have nothing else to brag

216 This refers to the appearance of Soviet bomber planes on April 10, 1944, indeed more than two months before June 17–19. They were on their way to bomb East Prussia and were heard in Vilna for hours; Kruk, *The Last Days*, p. 511.

about. They promise more inventions. For my sake, I hope they run out of time to do that.

I am far from being a political expert, but it seems to me that the fact that they have focused so much on England is actually a good thing. If the English also feel it, then maybe this will inflame them, and they will act to end the war more quickly. There are appeals, in bold type and in large letters on all four pages of the newspaper, for people to go to Germany to work there and in this way contribute to the fight against Bolshevism.

June 27 [1944].

Yesterday evening, when she served me my supper, the Christian woman brought me a piece of news. The front is now quite near, she said. The Soviets have crossed the Dvina River and they will be here soon.[217] She often brings me this type of news. Half a year ago, she told me that the Soviets were in Minsk and that they were expected to be in Vilna shortly.[218] Still, I always receive this news with joy. Whatever the truth may actually be, the fact is that somewhere they have broken through the front and are coming closer.

I couldn't fall asleep. All night long the trains were rumbling by and whistling. This is not the first time that the trains run day and night nonstop. Each time, I have the same thoughts: Maybe this time it's finally true? Maybe the Germans are really withdrawing? I become nervous and impatient. It would be better just to stick to my timetable. I just don't want to have to prolong it. And if it turns out to be sooner, then that will certainly be good. Regardless of what happens, I'll just continue to push the months further. I just hope that there won't be any disruptions.

A few days ago, my landlady again went into her "song and dance routine." I was already expecting it. It always happens at the end of the

---

217 Dvina River (today the Daugava or Western Dvina River) is a large river that rises in the Russian Valdai Hills and flows into the Riga Gulf of the Baltic Sea; it is more than 1,000 kilometers long. The diarist is referring here to Operation Bagration, the Soviet Byelorussian offensive operation, which began on the night of June 22–23, 1944, and resulted in the biggest defeat in German military history. Two days after it began, on June 24, the Russians pushed the German 9th Corps over the Dvina.

218 The distance between Minsk and Vilna is less than 200 kilometers.

month. She had skipped the previous month. Again the same story: She has kept me on too long and she gets no benefit from it. She is keeping me free of charge. She gets nothing from it. And, by the way, as always, [she recounts] a story that partisans had captured a large group of Jews and murdered them all. According to her stories, they have already murdered more Jews than there ever were altogether in the region.

She is trying to scare me. She doesn't understand that she can't frighten me with such tales. I have lived through too much. I have confronted death right under my nose too often. Even today, I am far from feeling safe and I am always prepared for anything. I don't deny it, I want very much to stay alive. I will always seek to avoid death. But I have already become so accustomed to it in my mind that I am not at all intimidated by it.

In normal circumstances, a human being thinks only about life. Seldom does he ever think about death. With me, it's just the opposite. Apparently, I am supposed to die, but it could happen that I will remain alive.

At the end of her entire lecture, I thanked her for sheltering me for such a long time and responded to her by saying that if she didn't want me, I would go away. I would not force myself on her. If she had pushed me to leave, I would have forked over to her something or other from the few things that I still have. Where could I have wandered about in the village? I know that she doesn't need more than this. She just wants me to keep on giving her things.

Yet right away she changed her tone and began to talk about other things, just like nothing had happened. In truth, I am a good business for her. And since things are now quiet—no house searches are going on—she will certainly not let me go. She is putting on this act to keep me scared. But I am glad that I can stay. I only hope that it stays this way until the liberation. As long as there are no more disturbances, she will probably be quiet through the end of next month. So, in the meantime, I don't have to think about it.

When I was in the ghetto, I could not at all conceive of where I would find a place to hide, or how I would get there. At that time, Jews were detained whenever they were on the roads. In such situations, you didn't dare to think about it too much nor make plans. You had to rely on fate.

June 30 [1944].

Today I read a newspaper again, this one dated June 28. The newspaper has made me happy. They write that furious battles are underway on all fronts with many losses on both sides. This is the first time that I've read such a comment. They admit that they are retreating, adding, however, that every advance of 1 kilometer by the enemy is only achieved with great difficulty. And, as though trying to justify this, they write that the Soviet summer offensive is characterized by an unlimited number of soldiers and war materiel being sent to the front as had never been done until now. And they keep on increasing the numbers. Because of this, they write that people should expect the nearest battles to move to new strategic locations. They report that they are bombing England ceaselessly—with their new bombs—weapons of revenge, as they call them. But these articles lack the enthusiasm of the earlier stories. As usual, there is some incitement against the Soviets. They cannot forgive Roosevelt for giving the Soviets a free hand. He did this, they write, to ensure that the Communists would vote for him in the coming elections. "Had it not been for the German resistance, he would have let Stalin destroy Europe." The Germans are the defenders of Europe! What a laugh! As far as I'm concerned, they can babble on about whatever they want, if they would only get out of here. This newspaper truly gave me hope. If things continue in this way, the Soviets presumably will arrive during the summer months.

Today, for some reason, there are no airplanes flying. I know that this doesn't mean anything. But I still want them to keep on droning and pounding.

July 1 [1944].

Today is Shabbat, the first of the seventh month. Altogether, there are five Shabbats, until the end of the month. And as I always do at the beginning of every month, I am already waiting for it to end quickly. As always, I am hoping that maybe this month will bring some news.

The more hopeful I become, the more impatient I become. I want to see freedom already...

Lately, as soon as it becomes light, around 2 A.M., I crawl out of my lair and walk around a bit, back and forth in the barn. I peek through a hole in the door. Before me is a superb thick forest. Nearby is a field where the rye has already grown very tall. All around, everything is green and fresh and fragrant with life. My heart grows heavy, I choke up, and I can't hold back the tears…

In the past, I would spend every summer day when I was free [from work] in the forest and the fields. The forest evokes so many memories! It's better not to look anymore. I should look at the bit of hay that I have here around me instead.

As soon as the sun begins to rise, I go back to hide in my lair. Soon things begin to stir. The first person to go out is the old lady who lets out the chickens. I look through the little crack. It's interesting to watch the chickens run out. The rooster is the first one out, running quickly, as if he was late for something. I have never seen such a beautiful rooster. His comb shines from afar. He is white, his wings spattered with various colors, tall and lean. After him, the chickens run out majestically. Each one lovelier than the other. Various colors. They run around all day. First of all, they run into the barn. They know, however, that they will be chased out of there. All you have to say is "*Akish*," and they run out right away. The rooster displays a distinct antipathy toward one of the chickens. She is in fact the ugliest one. As soon as he encounters her, he attacks her. And she tries to get away from him. In this way, they get along in their own little world…

After letting out the chickens, the landlady leads out the horses and ties them up somewhere so that they can graze. At one time, all horses looked the same to me.[219] Here, through the little peephole, I first began to make distinctions and notice that there are beautiful horses and ugly ones. She then leads out the cows and milks them in the yard. Whenever a cow stubbornly resists and won't let herself be milked, she hits it and curses it. In general, she talks to the animals just as if they could understand

---

219 The diarist refers to the episode near Niementchin when, after running away from the ghetto, she was asked by the villagers about the kind of horse that the Lithuanian wagon-owner who had given her the address had; she could not answer this question.

what she is saying. After that, the young Christian girl comes out with two pails to get water from the pump.

She comes here to the barn with a basket to get some potatoes and, at the same time, she takes several pieces of wood to burn in the oven in order to cook breakfast. The men have already gone out. Today they are cutting. I saw them taking scythes along. About three hours later, the Christian woman comes out with a pail, so I know that she is bringing me my breakfast. She puts the pot of food and the plate into the pail so that no one will notice. I immediately begin to estimate how much time remains until lunch. And at lunchtime I calculate how long it will be until supper. This is how it's been from the very first day. It isn't because of my appetite, but rather to get through the day more quickly. When she brings me supper, that means the day has ended. Even in the winter, when this happens at 4 or 5 P.M., I consider the day to be over.

It seems like all I think about all day long is eating.

In this way, the life I lead is totally like that of a beast, like the cow that stands here and chews grass. In addition, there is also the squeaking of the mice. They really are quite a nuisance. They slither around here, free as they please, and I am in perpetual fear that at any moment now they are about to crawl on me. Sometimes a couple of cats come in here and they meow with such whining cries that they actually would scare me, until I finally got used to it. When I first got here, I used to think that a young Christian boy was poking around here and I trembled with fear that he might discover me.

It's interesting that even cats have intelligence. When they want to climb up high, above the stall that is next to me, they go to the ladder and climb up on it, just like humans. They keep an eye out to see when I get my food. At dinnertime, they spring up on me and then they wait for me to give them something to eat.

A curious thing happened to me because of the cats. It was already dark and I had jumped down from my hiding place. At that time it was situated way up high, almost to the roof. Something started to move toward the wall. To me, it seemed as if someone was there. It just so happened that around that time, I had experienced several scares. Just the day before, the landlord, not knowing that I was here, was looking for something in the barn. He had a *kolkhoz* woman with him who was staying with them at the time. The Christian woman had told me that this woman was very curious to know everything and that she never misses anything. I became very frightened. As it is, I am always afraid here. In the dark, everything appears different to me. I began to think: what should I do? If I were to spend the night [here] and something were to happen, I would be in a trap. But if I would leave, I would have a chance to escape. In a panic, I climbed back up to my [hiding] place, put on my fur jacket, wrapped myself in my shawl, put on my felt boots, gathered up all my belongings, and climbed down. It still seemed to me that someone was moving about [in the barn]. I went out. I even wanted to tell the Christian woman that somebody was in the barn. But I held back. There would have been an uproar and then I would not have been able to remain here any longer. I moved into a corner where no one could see me and waited to see if anyone would come out of the barn. Every step that I took echoed with the sound of crunching snow, so I was afraid to make the slightest move. Sitting there like that, I began to reassess the situation. If someone had wanted to detain me, he would have detained me. He would not have let me go out and would have made himself known right away. On the other hand, if someone had wanted to hide himself, then he would have certainly become frightened and would have run away immediately. This means that it was all in my imagination.

I was pleased that I had controlled myself and had not caused a commotion. Still, I sat and watched. Perhaps someone was there after all? Quite a while later, a cat came out through a hole. It was [the sound of] her moving around in the straw that had frightened me. In spite of how sad my heart felt, I just had to burst out laughing. Today I realize how comical that whole scene must have seemed.

My nerves were always so much on edge that every little thing scared me. Even if a chicken came into the barn or a bird would fly in, I would become afraid. I was constantly listening for noises and was always stressed out lest someone might discover me here. Lately I've calmed down a bit. First of all, they now lock the barn every night with a key. The *kolkhoz* woman is gone. That is a big deal for me. Because of her, I was always terrified. Even the old man now knows about me, so I am no longer afraid of him. Because he's an old man, I didn't think that he could hear anything, but he has a sharp eye. If the straw was spread out even just a little bit differently, he would notice it right away and would ask who had been there. It was because of him that I had been forced to move to a different place. Apparently, they have now told him about me because they no longer hide things from him. They bring me food even if he is in the barn. It is much more comfortable for me that everyone who comes in here knows about me. In general, they come in here less often than they did in the winter, and far less often than in the autumn. Then they would spend whole days in here: threshing, cutting chaff, coming in all the time to get hay for the cattle, or to lay straw on the ground.

I feel the most comfortable, however, when no one is here. Overall, things have recently become better for me in all respects. Through the crack, I see who comes in and out, so I don't have to wonder whether someone is there or not. For hours at a time, I stand, leaning over, peering through the crack—if you stand upright, you can't see. I observe who comes to visit the Christian woman, and when someone leaves the house, I await their return, as if this was of great importance to me.

I try to distract myself with all sorts of nonsense to occupy my mind and to keep me from worrying about anything else. It seems to me that I am succeeding. I don't think about anything, everything is forgotten. But I only need to doze a bit, sometimes even that's not necessary, and then I see before me various faces, often distant acquaintances with whom I seldom got together, occasionally even people whom I only knew by sight. It all becomes a confused muddle before my eyes and I wake up with a start: they are all gone, all annihilated, and in what manner!

When slaughtering an animal, care is taken so that it suffers as little as possible. With us, it was exactly the opposite. They went out of their way to torment us as much as possible. I strenuously push away these thoughts. It is unbearable to think about it. But, how do you find a way to truly forget it?

Just recently, I saw in my mind's eye a group of people, whose faces I recognized; one of whom, Magun, was their leader. They ran through Mickiewicz Street, and at his command, all of them, raising their hands called out: "Long live the Red Army!" Then they scattered in all directions to hide. The police chased them. I was one of them and I ran into a Christian confectionery [shop].

July 4 [1944].

Yesterday, all day long, without a stop, the airplanes droned on. Every once in a while, you heard explosions. In the middle of the night, you could hear many powerful bombs exploding. The Christian woman told me today that the Soviets are already in Old Vileika,[220] and that the Germans are withdrawing from Niementchin and are not letting anyone in or out. They are preparing to burn down the town.[221] How she knows what they plan to do, I can't even begin to understand. According to her, the Lithuanians in Vilna are selling everything and running away. And last night, the Soviets dropped incendiary bombs on Vilna, and all of Vilna is in flames.

I don't know what part of this is true. I see, however, that things seem to be stirring up. She went on to say that the Soviets will be coming here, but that the government will be an English one. This is already pure gibberish. Are the Soviets going to allow themselves to be led around by the nose? They [the Poles], however, dream that England will establish an [independent] Poland for them.[222] They are also placing their hopes on the Polish partisans.

Today, for some reason, it's actually quiet. It's a beautiful, sunny day. There isn't even the slightest breeze. The cattle are far away somewhere. You don't hear any mooing. The dogs are quiet. The rooster was slaughtered the very next morning after I had admired him. All you hear are the birds. A long time ago such stillness gave me pleasure. It was the best relaxation. But today my heart isn't in it. A rebellion stirs up within me. I wish only that there be lots of noise and pounding, that there be bombing, burning, annihilating, killing. I myself would have volunteered to lend a hand and would have found satisfaction in doing so.

The old woman was just here. She sat down next to me for a brief visit. She says that it is now safe for me to crawl out of my lair, that the Soviets will be here today or tomorrow.

---

220 Old Vileika or Vileika is a town about 120 kilometers east of Vilna. The Red Army recaptured the town on July 2, 1944.

221 Niementchin was recaptured by the Soviets on July 7, 1944.

222 This may be a reference to the Polish government-in-exile, which was based in London.

Is this really true? It's hard for me to believe. My heart begins to beat more quickly. I have been waiting for this moment for so long. And yet at the same time I am afraid of it. What will I do? Which way should I turn? To whom? I believe it was Lermontov who wrote somewhere: "*Chto den griadushchiy mne gatovit*"?[223] I ask myself the same question: What does fate have in store for me? You want so much to still see good things happening.

My desires are not at all very great. I want only to have a tranquil life, without aggravation. I cannot imagine what that will look like. But it does happen that the impossible becomes possible. Who could have ever imagined it to be possible that in one day, not even twenty-four hours, all of Vilna's Jews could be confined in one little corner? And then that in the course of two years Vilna would be completely "liberated" of such a dense, well-established Jewish population that had been there for hundreds of years?[224] If that can happen, then it could also happen that something, which today seems impossible to me, might become possible. I must believe this and not question it.

I only know that I have not yet gotten anything out of life. I consider life to be in my debt in a very big way. I would very much like, at least in the second half of my life, to collect payment for this debt. If indeed I live to see the Soviets and crawl out of here to the free world, then I must completely make myself over, wipe out entirely all sentimental feeling. I have to forget everything and everyone, just as if nothing and nobody had ever existed in the world until now. I have to accept everything with a good-natured spirit, without a sense of tragedy. Only in this way is it possible for me to continue to exist. It is a difficult task, and I have doubts as to whether I can pull it off.

---

223 This phrase in Russian means: This day to come, what will it bring? It is actually from Alexander Pushkin's novel in verse, *Eugene Onegin*, chap. 6, stanza 21; https://www.poetryintranslation.com/PITBR/Russian/Onegin6.php (accessed January 10, 2023).

224 The diarist refers to the two years from the establishment of the Vilna ghetto on September 6, 1941, to its liquidation on September 23–24, 1943.

July 5 [1944].

I have already taken my stroll around the barn and am back in my [hiding] place. Today, the weather is again gorgeous. Could it be that I will yet be able to enjoy summer? Last night airplanes flew by again, very near, passing overhead. But I did not hear any bomb explosions. Before, I used to hear some shooting. Now, apparently, they are no longer shooting at the planes. Today it is quiet again. It makes me nervous. It's already been a few days that you don't even hear the trains. I am waiting for breakfast. Yesterday, the Christian traveled to the mill. Perhaps they will have some news to tell me.

July 6 [1944].

Yesterday, at nightfall, a panic broke out here. Someone had arrived, riding on a horse and announced that, several kilometers from here, Germans had turned up and were setting fire to everything. So some of the Christians in the region banded together and went to stop them. Everyone was walking around in tears, carrying their belongings, and preparing to save themselves. It turned out that they were only forty Latvians who were just passing by. But everybody got stressed out. People are saying that Podbrodzh[225] and several other places have been set on fire. This must also be a lie.

They have already brought the clover in from the field. It has a pleasant, fresh fragrance. At daybreak, I crawled way up high and, through a hole, I saw two airplanes. They looked like two little birds, but because of their droning sound, I knew that these were airplanes. I wished them all the success in the world. In previous times, I would have wondered if the planes were German or Soviet. Now I am sure that they are Soviet.

When we were still in the ghetto, all of us had waited for them with such great longing.[226] But the vast majority did not live to see them. They kept us waiting for too long.

---

225 This town is located 47 kilometers northeast of Vilna and 25 kilometers northeast of Niementchin.

226 Kruk mentioned Soviet airplanes over Vilna on January 25–26, 1943; Kruk, *The Last Days*, p. 454.

It has occurred to me that at this moment, while they are flying overhead and dropping their bombs, all of us, our tiny handful of survivors, scattered in various holes, are united in one emotion of joy and hope.

Since yesterday, also in the middle of the night, they have flown over many times, apparently going back and forth. And because it has also been thundering, I haven't been able to distinguish between the bombs and the thunder. I am just waiting for more and more bombs, for greater and greater destruction. I would really like to know precisely where the Soviets are!

The Christians say that the Niementchin *gmina* ran away,[227] that the Lithuanians looted everything there, but that the Polish partisans overtook them on the road and took everything away from them, leaving them standing in their underwear, even with their buttons torn off, so they say. They also relate that the Lithuanians killed a large group of Polish children in some village. So the partisans have just set off for Lithuania to take revenge. This pleases me to no end. Let them take each other's heads off. That will leave us with a few less "good friends."

There really aren't any partisans coming through here anymore. People are saying that the trains are not running at all. Indeed, it has already been several days since I've heard their rumbling. It is possible that this is actually true because last night Latvians dressed in German uniforms commandeered about forty coachmen and ordered them to drive. These Latvians had to flee from the Soviet occupied areas and head for Latvia. One of the young men here was also forced to go.[228] They [his family] are worried that something might happen to him on the way. I myself am also hoping that he returns unharmed.

The airplanes are circling all the time. It seems that their base is nearby. They load up here and fly on. Apparently, they are dropping the bombs somewhere further away. I have heard bombs dropping only a few times around here. Just now, at this very moment, there was a really big blast, very appropriately!

---

227 It refers to the Niementchin Municipality. A *gmina* is the smallest Polish territorial unit of administration.

228 This refers to the younger son of the Christian farmwoman, as clearly indicated further.

The Christian woman just came by and said that the Soviets are already in Niementchin, but I don't believe it.[229] So what. I have the patience to wait another few days. If they aren't here yet, obviously, they will arrive soon.

July 7 [1944].

All night long and even now, airplanes are continuously flying. You often hear powerful explosions, as well as heavy shooting. This means that the Germans are still here, contrary to what the neighbors are saying, that they have gone.

You can feel the concentrated, intensive effort that is being brought to bear in this area. Maybe these are the final decisive bombs that I have been waiting for all this time. But until I see for myself at least one Red Army soldier, I will not believe it.

Everybody is still sleeping. Perhaps, there will be some news today.

July 8 [1944].

Here it is, Shabbat again. Another week pushed through. After yesterday, it seems to me that by next Shabbat, I will finally be able to crawl out of this hole. I am completely happy about yesterday. At this moment, you could not have wished for a better day. The airplanes circled nonstop, one sortie after another. Bombs poured down just like hailstones, especially during the first half of the day. The whole barn literally shook several times. It is very likely that they are escorting the Germans out with blasts somewhere near the main road. Three years ago, on June 22, 1941, the Germans escorted the Soviets out in a similar manner. But the world turns and it has now turned for so long that it has finally turned all the way around.

Today, airplanes are flying around again, and explosions can be heard, which means that we are still not finished with the Germans.

---

229 The Russian army recaptured the town on July 7, 1944.

The Christians are saying that Soviets were seen driving around in trucks yesterday. The *kolkhozniks* who are in the neighboring villages are also waiting impatiently for the Soviets to arrive.[230] They too are broken people: they were taken from their homes and ruined. But there is no comparison with us. They are here with their families, with their wives, husbands, and children. They move about freely among the local inhabitants.

Materialistic issues are certainly among the most important aspects of life. But they are not of eternal concern. As long as a person is alive, he can hope that the world turns for him as well, and so things can turn around. But for us, the rotation of the world cannot help any more. The Ponary dead will not come back to life…

It is 6 A.M. Just now, looking through the crack in the wall, I saw five Red Army soldiers. They went into the Christian woman's house and came out with a loaf of bread and a pitcher of milk. I heard them say, "*Balshoye spasiba*."[231] Now that I have finally seen them with my very own eyes, I have to believe it.

Airplanes are heard less often and only lone planes are flying. No bombs are being dropped. It is very likely that they are already in Vilna. I should be rejoicing, but a kind of heaviness presses in on me and I cannot…

It grieves me that at such a moment, which I have been waiting for so impatiently and with such longing for three full years, none of my near and dear ones remain with whom to celebrate.

I am not going to crawl out of my hole yet. I am disappointed with myself: I thought I had made an agreement with myself, no sentimentalism, and here, at the first test, I have failed. I can't stop crying. But it's pointless. I have to control myself. I would love to get so drunk now until I forget everything.

---

230 *Kolkhozniks* here probably refers to Russian farmers from the Soviet Union who lived in the Vilna region before and during the war.

231 This phrase in Russian means: Thank you very much.

I will have to make sure that I am always among people, never alone with my own thoughts. Today it is 286 days that I have been alone.[232] You can really get sick of yourself in the course of such a long period…

I actually had a bit of a laugh yesterday. The bees suddenly started buzzing around and a whole army of them came swarming down. There was a hoo-ha. Everybody in the house came running out with pails of water and brooms, and sprayed them to make them go away. The old man put some kind of rag on his head and ran around back and forth, covering his ears with his hands. The son wrapped a towel around his head and ears, and put on a heavy jacket, buttoned up to the neck. Apparently, he wanted to take a look at the beehives to see what had happened. But as soon as he got close, he immediately fell to his knees and covered his face.

The younger brother, the one who was taken away by the Latvians, was the one who usually took care of the bees. He would do the job quietly and without a fuss. He would simply put a net over his face and deal with them without anybody's help. And now they even had to call a neighbor to help, and all of them together couldn't cope with the situation. It's a true proverb that says "*Diela mastera baitsa*."[233]

The Christians, whom the Latvians had taken away, went as far as Malat,[234] where they then dispersed the horses and returned on foot. Some of them were reluctant to leave their horses behind and continued further [with the Latvians], but a few hours later, they too escaped. They were supposed to have taken the Latvians all the way to Latvia.

The old woman came running right away to share the news with me that her son was back. I am truly very happy. He had been in great danger because of both the Lithuanians and the bombardments. After all that they have done for me, I am a true and good friend to them and wish them only well. It is quite possible that were it not for them, I might not be here anymore. The old woman apparently believes that I have a special merit with God, so she asks me to help her pray to God. Her main concerns are

---

232 The diarist entered the barn on September 27, 1943; that is, 286 days before the date of this entry, July 8, 1944.

233 This Russian phrase means: The work is afraid of the master. That is, for a true master, nothing is impossible. He will always find a way out of a difficult situation. This Russian idiomatic expression is used to praise a craftsman who has finished a good piece of work.

234 Malat is 50 kilometers north of Niementchin, a distance of about ten hours by foot.

her children. Can I then refuse her? She would be greatly disappointed if I told her that I had no contact with God.

July 9 [1944].

Today Mitya was here.[235] I had actually figured out that today was exactly the day that he would be coming. I could hardly wait to see him. We talked and we talked and we never finished. Is it possible to talk so much that you run out of words? It seems to me that I will be able to talk about this for the rest of my life, repeating it endlessly over and over again, and it will always still be fresh in my memory. Now suddenly I feel like I am being lifted up in the air. I cannot sit anymore. If only I had someone here with me with lots of patience so that I could talk and talk without stopping. Just to talk things out after so many months. How do you wait for the moment when we, this handful of survivors, can gather together? I feel so close to each and every one of them, even those I don't know. After so much suffering, we have to be very close, to be connected.

I still can hardly believe that it is all over. Let it not be just a dream. That would be terrible!

July 10 [1944].

Bathing is still a sore issue for me. It's not as bad as before, but I still have not gotten to the point of being able to bathe every day as people normally do. Yesterday in the evening, totally unexpectedly, they brought me a full tub of water and a bowl. Even the old woman helped. Lately, she has begun to address me with the title *Pani*.[236] Before, she used to call me *kobieta* and *te*.[237] This title is really very important to me!

Early in the morning, I crawled out and bathed properly. I also washed out all my things, even my autumn coat, albeit in cold water but

---

235 Mitya was the youngest son of the Christian farmwoman.

236 This is a respectful form of address in Polish, which means: Madame.

237 The Polish word *kobieta* (woman) was considered derogatory until the nineteenth century. The Polish word *ty* is the second person, singular form of the pronoun you.

nonetheless water. I will try to ask them if perhaps they could again bring me at least a bowl of water this evening. I would gladly give up a meal just to have the chance to wash myself.

Airplanes have been flying around all morning, and you hear loud explosions and heavy shooting. I am no longer happy about these bombs. They are very likely German bombs. It seems logical to me that they can no longer turn back. Of course, they could come here, even from Berlin, to drop their bombs. This would only cause devastation, more victims. However, this has no decisive significance in times of war. Here they are, bombing England, and they don't even have any intention of invading it.

The Christians are saying that the Soviets have only barely broken through and that the actual front is still far away.[238] Even if that is so, they did not, after all, come here just for laughs and they will not let themselves be pushed back. If I ever thought that this could actually happen, then I would not stay here but would go to them and ask them to take me with them, even to the front. But I cannot believe that will happen. Yet who knows? Many illogical things are happening, especially in these times. I am overcome with dread. Let the war end soon, otherwise we will never have any rest here at all!

July 11 [1944].

Last night, they brought me some political news. The Germans are sending troops into Vilna. One person said 7,000 and another said 70,000. Apparently, the addition or omission of a zero makes no difference [to the person]. I, for one, consider both numbers to be absurd. Even if they are sending in troops, it cannot be such a large number. Besides Vilna, they have lost many other cities, so why would they single out Vilna to direct

238 By the beginning of July, the front line had been breached, roughly on a line from Vitebsk to Vilna. Indeed, a large part of the Soviet force was employed to reduce the German pocket east of Minsk, but the Soviet High Command decided to turn mobile formations toward the major traffic center of Vilna. The Soviet 5th Guards Tank Army encircled the city from the south on July 8, 1944, and trapped the garrison.

so much power at it? The fact that they are already talking about troops makes me believe that Vilna is already in Soviet hands.[239]

Airplanes are flying around nonstop, but you don't hear any bomb explosions. So these are probably Soviet planes. My nerves are tense to the breaking point. I can no longer control them. I don't know what to do with them. If I only had a cigarette, it would be much easier for me. But I have nowhere [to turn] to arrange this. If I ask the Christians for one, they will look at me strangely. After all, they cannot understand this. I have held out this long, so I just have to hang on a little longer.

I am waiting impatiently for the young man with whom I fled from here into the forest six and a half months ago, because of the *burlaks*.[240] We lived through a very difficult moment then. Even though he knew all the people around here, still, I understand, that even for him it was not easy to ask to be taken in. But I had absolutely no one to ask. I often think of him and recall that night. The rumor around here is that he was killed. But Mitya says that he knows for sure that he is alive. I only hope that it is so. The hope, after all, is that at least those who managed to break away from the Germans should remain alive. The Polish partisans, as it is, have also slaughtered enough of them. I believe that if he is alive then he will be coming here any day now. He is probably also interested in knowing if I am alive. The fact that he hasn't come yet probably means that it is not yet safe to go out.

The Christians have offered to have me stay in their house. But I am still holding back. I am no longer afraid for myself, but there are gangs of thugs roaming around, and I wouldn't want my benefactors to have any trouble on my account. It's better to wait a few more days when some authority will probably be established.

I look for ways to shorten the days. They brought me some medical literature to read. But I have to reread it from the beginning several times before I am finally able to concentrate. One professor writes here that

239 The writer was partially right; on July 11, 1944, the Soviets were still fighting their way into Vilna in intense street-by-street fighting.

240 This refers to Eliash, the Jewish acquaintance of the peasant family who was also in hiding and who, together with the diarist, was discovered and had to flee to the forest on December 22, 1943.

by self-suggestion, a person can be in total control of himself and even heal the worst illness. All you need is to have a strong will. In certain situations, I agree with him. Here I am, keeping myself together for almost ten months through [the power of] suggestion. It is interesting that many of the methods that he presents are the ones that I myself have used. Which means that it wasn't as idiotic as I thought. For example, he says that to calm your nerves, you should count mechanically. I would count for hours on end, counting into the thousands. And I would sing to myself. I would listen to some kind of monotonous sound, like the ticking of a clock or, as I used to do, to the mooing of a cow or the chirping of the birds. In general, I would focus my attention on the greatest nonsense, and in this way I could avoid thinking about upsetting matters. Now, however, I can no longer use these methods. It makes me even more nervous. I am looking for a different technique. I can't sit down at all, so instead I stand. Early in the morning, I crawl out and before things get going, I walk around, I run around, I climb onto the hay that is stacked way up high and I jump from one end to the other. I even do gymnastics. If anyone were to see me then, they would surely think I had lost my mind. I seem perfectly normal to myself, although a crazy person never recognizes his own craziness. However, from the first day on, I have maintained control of myself. Even the Christians often tell me that it is a wonder I did not go mad, having been alone for such a long time. This is certainly proof that I am normal. Also, my writing has brought me a certain relief. I don't think about what to write. I just hack away with whatever comes to mind. It may well be that I have written such foolish stories so many times that if I ever have the occasion someday to read it over, I myself will have to laugh. In the meantime, a little more time passes, and for me, that is the most important thing.

July 12 [1944].

Last night I got a real shower. The more time that passes, the worse the roof leaks. Right now, it is another beautiful, sunny morning. Maybe the next time it rains, I will be under a real roof! It also thundered very loudly. I thought that the thunder would come right in here at any moment. That would have been totally unjust. Now I most certainly want to live. It so happens that in a village not too far from here, there was actually a fire.

Yesterday, starting in the second half of the day, you could hear loud explosions and often heavy shooting. It still isn't over. The Christians say that London Radio reported that Polish partisans helped [the Soviets] to occupy Vilna.

The old woman just came in and asked me if I had been frightened by the thunder. She is very attentive to me. She says that several bombs fell in Niementchin. At this very moment the pounding continues.

July 13 [1944].

Today is the third anniversary of the day that they took Tzalel away. The more time that passes, the closer I come to realizing that I cannot continue to hope that he is still alive. The Germans are not leaving any Jews behind as they retreat. In Vilna, the day before they withdrew, they slaughtered the last remnant of Jews who were still living in the blocks.[241] And even if he [Tzalel] had somehow managed to escape, how could he have held out these three years. And yet I still think to myself: maybe?

I believe that those who were taken away to Estonia are no longer alive. I am sorry about Felman. He actually could have saved himself [after running away] from the ghetto, but he made a blunder. This man, in his time, saved my life. I would be very happy if I still had an opportunity to thank him.

Last night, I dreamed again about a whole succession of acquaintances. I carried on a conversation with them, some kind of confused muddle. I woke up with a heavy heart. I still cannot get used to the idea that all of them are dead.

Today, so far, it is completely quiet, no airplanes and no bombs. Yesterday, the Christians told me that there are still Germans in Vilna.

---

241 The Kailis and H.K.P. blocks, populated by less than 2,500 Jews, were liquidated on July 2–3, 1944, ten days before the Red Army marched in and captured the city toward the evening of July 13.

They are at Schlossbarg with lots of ammunition,[242] and furthermore, 28,000 Polish partisans are helping to fight against them. Why should it bother the Soviets? It certainly doesn't bother me. After the way they treated us, especially these last few months, may their heads roll in the same manner that they took ours.

July 14 [1944].

Yesterday, for the first time during all this time, I spoke with the old landlord. I was sitting down, not hidden away in my hole as I usually am, and talked with the old man. When he came in this time, I didn't hide myself as I had always done before, and greeted him, "good morning." He responded, "*Chotch raz pokazalasya*."[243] He recalled how, together with the *kolkhoz* woman, he had searched in the straw; he himself was afraid at that moment, thinking that a soldier or even a thief was hiding there—isn't that ironic. I was sitting there trembling with fear, and they were afraid of me; how he had found a piece of bread and butter in the neighbor's barn, where I was staying at the time, and told people to search through the straw to see if anyone was hiding there; how he would notice the spread out straw, until finally, in the end, he found out about me. He is amazed at how I managed to survive for such a long time in the barn, especially during the winter months. I myself don't know how I survived. My hands and feet became frozen. Even now, they give me sharp, stabbing pains. But it could have been much worse. The realization that I had no choice and my strong will helped me to survive. From the very first day, I set myself a goal never to let anyone from the village see me and to sit it out with these Christians until the end. For that reason, I declined to go to the house of one of their acquaintances where they wanted to set me up. I understood that no one would keep me for very long in a house. At that time, everyone was jittery because of [Polish]

---

242 This refers to the Castle Hill, which dominates Vilna. The first castle there was built around 1323 by the Lithuanian Grand Duke Gediminas (1275–1341), who declared Vilna as the capital of Lithuania.

243 This Russian expression means: So finally, you show yourself.

partisans. If this is really the end, then I have succeeded. None of the people around here know about me.

July 15 [1944].

One should never become too cocky. Yesterday, I missed being discovered by a hair's breadth. Without any warning, they took down the roof to fix it. I was left exposed under the open sky. If it had only been my own people, but instead it was a *kolkhoznik* who had come along to help. I moved back as far as I could deep into my lair. He was about to remove some of the straw, and after taking down a few bundles, he would have immediately seen me. Nowadays I am not really in any danger, but it would have seemed strange to him. After all, this would have certainly caused a sensation. He would have spread the story all over the whole region.

My usual approach is the fewer the number of people who know about something, even nonsense, the better off I am. So I was really quite upset. It annoyed me that right at the very end I had slipped up. But even this time, things worked out all right for me. The old woman came by. Apparently, she had not known [about the roof repair] in advance. She called everyone away to eat, and then came back alone and helped me to move to another spot.

I have been sitting in this hole for seventy-two days, surrounded by all the "comforts of home."[244] I had thought that I would not have to move again and that when I finally crawled out to freedom, it would be from here. The truth is that I could have crawled out already by now, but I don't have any place or any person that I need to rush to get to. Let it quiet down a little bit. I don't want to just hang around in the village. People would now look at me [a live Jew] in amazement, just as if I was some kind of rare, wild beast that had run away from a dense forest. Besides that, there are still thugs roaming around. It's better to stay here a little longer, instead of taking a chance that I might have to crawl around again. Now I find myself in the exact same spot that I crawled into on the first

---

244 Seventy two days before this entry was written was May 5, 1944, ten days before the writer began her diary. It is not clear what happened on this day.

day that I came here and where I stayed for sixty-eight days.[245] This time I won't have to stay that long.

Each time that I move, I make myself "comfortable" right away. From here, I can no longer see what the Christians are doing. But if I remove a whole board, I have before me a pretty view: the sky, the trees, and the fields.

July 17 [1944].

I came within a hair's breadth of going to Vilna today. Both of the young Christians were going there and they invited me to come along. But I kept myself from rushing off. To see the corpses laid out in the streets? My nerves are too weak for that. I'm not worried about being too late to see the devastation.

A heaviness presses in on me. How does one start life all over again? Loneliness terrifies me. Where to go? What to do? Maybe I will find acquaintances, friends. But that's not it. I know how it feels to be among people and yet feel lonely. I don't need much. I just need one person…

July 19 [1944].

I think that today is my last day in the barn. I have finally decided to go to Vilna tomorrow on a scouting trip. When all is said and done, you have to crawl out eventually. I have been sitting like this almost two weeks too long. After all that I've been through, I should be totally unemotional. And yet, I cannot control myself. My heart is soaring in the air. Lately, I can't even fall asleep.

[End of diary]

---

245 The amount of time that the diarist specifies here is not accurate; she arrived there on September 27, 1943, and moved to the farmwoman's home on December 5, 1943, seventy—not sixty-eight—days later.

Ruth Leimenzon Engles' Biography

by Lazar Engles

Ruth was born in Vilna in 1915.[1] Her father, David Leimenzon, was a pharmacist and her mother, a midwife. Ruth received a Jewish national education. She had to interrupt her high school education at the Jewish Polish Gymnasium Oświata in Vilna,[2] because her parents could no longer afford the high tuition, and she had to go out and earn a living in her early youth.

Thanks to her father's business connections with a Polish wholesale cosmetic and pharmaceutical firm, she got a job, at first as an office worker and later as a representative in the city and in the province. Her boss, who belonged to the reactionary party of the Endeks,[3] was far from being a lover of Jews. However, he displayed tolerance and respect toward his Jewish employee, very likely because Ruth was capable and useful to his firm. Both her Polish boss and his wife behaved humanely at a time when the value of the human species had become so cheapened. Thanks to them, Ruth was saved from Ponary during the liquidation of the Vilna ghetto.

---

1 This year is inaccurate. According to all her vital records, she was born in 1910.

2 The coeducational Gymnasium Oświata (Enlightenment) was under the auspices of the Vilna Central Jewish Committee.

3 It refers to Narodowa Demokracja (National Democracy, known by its abbreviation, ND, and its members Endeks), a right-wing nationalist Polish party, which was known for its antisemitic stance to exclude Jews from economic life and to push them to emigration out of the country.

Two years before World War II,[4] Ruth married Tzalel Trakinski and was happy, but their joy did not last very long. A few days after the Germans brutally occupied Vilna at the end of June 1941, her husband was captured in the streets by the Lithuanian *chapunes*,[5] and she never saw him again.[6] Just before the liquidation of the ghetto in September 1943, with the help of her former boss's wife, she succeeded in making contact with a peasant family in the village of Simanuvka near the small town of Niementchin, 20 kilometers from Vilna, where she found a hiding place in a barn. She stayed there in the most appalling conditions, going many days without a bite to eat or drink.

It was her destiny to remain alive as the sole survivor of her murdered family. Broken, with frozen feet, after nearly a year lying in the barn, she lived to see the liberation and made her way back to Vilna. Not finding a relative or an acquaintance during the first days in desolate and devastated Jewish Vilna, she rejoiced to run into a longtime friend of her husband one day. On the next-to-last page of her diary, in which Ruth had written a page every day,[7] there is a short paragraph, which reads as follows:

> July 17, 1944…A heaviness presses in on me. How does one start life all over again? Loneliness terrifies me. Where to go? What to do? Maybe I will find acquaintances, friends. But that's not it. I know how it feels to be among people and yet feel lonely. I don't need much. I just need one person.

Ruth and I met unexpectedly on one of the devastated Vilna streets in 1944. She considered me to be the nearest [person] to her. That was natural. I had been her husband, Tzalel's, comrade since our school days.

---

4 Actually, it was less than one and a half years before World War II, but three years before Operation Barbarossa, the attack of the Germans on Soviet Lithuania.

5 The literal translation is "snatchers." These were especially Lithuanian nationalists—policemen, soldiers, and former members of the paramilitary Lithuanian Riflemen's Union—and all sorts of bandits in the service of the Germans, mostly members of the murderous Vilnian unit Ypatingasis būys.

6 This description does not match the description related in the diary. Ruth wrote there that her husband was seized on July 13, 1941 from their home and not from the street.

7 Since the end of June 1944, she added entries to the diary almost every day.

In April 1945, we left Vilna, and after months of wandering, we reached sunny, free Italy, where we got stuck in a refugee camp in Rome. In due time, we were blessed with a son and named him after Ruth's murdered father, David.

The camp conditions were far from ideal for family life. But Ruth was happy and lived with the hope of beginning a normal life. However, she did not have the strength to handle the joys of family under the given conditions. The effects of that difficult winter in the barn began to make themselves felt. Twice she needed to go to the hospital to undergo an operation, followed by convalescence at the Joint Sanitarium.

At the end of 1949, we went to the "Golden Land," and, with the help of my brother and Ruth's relatives, we began our renewed life in New York. I quickly found work as a compositor for the Yiddish newspaper *Tog* and earned enough to live on. It seemed that together with a normalized lifestyle, Ruth would grow stronger and would overcome her infirmities.

In 1953, Ruth experienced her first serious attack. We were on vacation in the Catskill Mountains at the time. From that time on, she began to consult with specialists, and underwent continual tests. In 1954 she underwent a serious operation and lay for weeks in the hospital. Little by little she began to heal and resumed housekeeping and the education of our child, who was now of school age. Nine months later, she again had to go to the hospital, where she lay for three months. In the summer of 1955, she breathed her last breath, at the age of forty.[8]

All these years, I have taken good care of the notebook, wanting to keep it with me until my son David was mature enough to be able to read it, and most important of all, to be able to understand what his mother had been through. I later decided to settle in Israel and to give the book over to the place where it belonged. Now, four years after my *aliya*, the time has come to publish this document.

---

8 This is inaccurate. Ruth was forty-five years old.

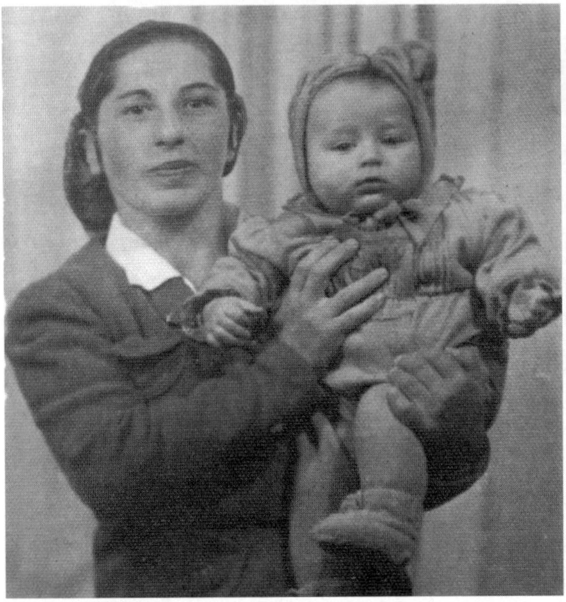

Ruth and her son, David, 1946, Cinecittà DP Camp, Rome, Italy.
Photo Archive, GFH, no. 37533.

Ruth and her son, David, 1954, New York, U.S.
Courtesy of David Engles.

Four generations of the Engles family at Eva and David Engles' 50th wedding anniversary celebration, Jerusalem, Israel 2021. Courtesy of the Engles family.

Index

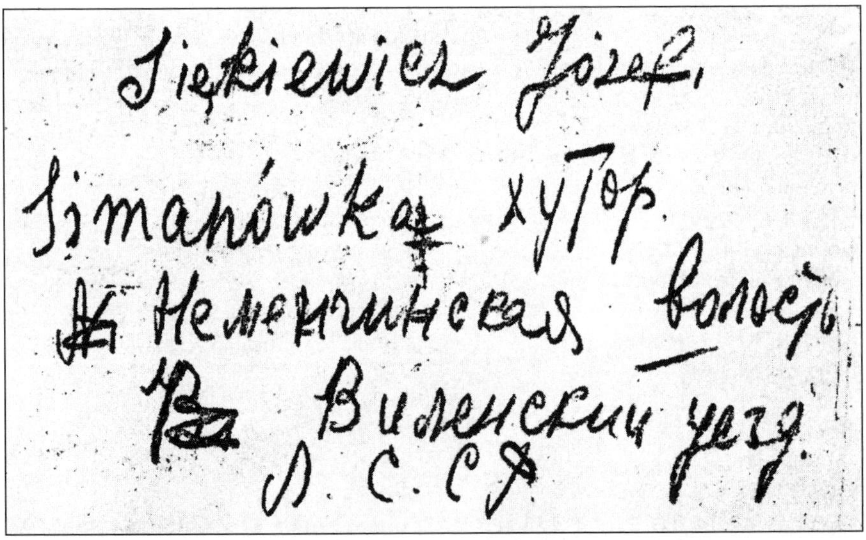
Siękiewicz Józef,
Simanówka хутор.
Немечинская волость
в Виленский уезд
Л.С.С.Р.

The name and address of Ruth Leimenzon's savior, as it appears on the last page of her diary.